Dearest Sharon,

Mahalo nui loa! Mahalagá ikaw! Salamat po para sa pagkakaibigan ikaw. You are definately the verb <u>love</u>. There's no end to action for you. You are inspiration to all who know you or even know of you.

Thank you again for allowing me to expose your many talents. This is such an exciting time. I did know the first time we met that Heavenly Father had some very big plans for you because of the big heart He gave you.

Aloha! + Mahalkita!

Suzanne

LOVE
IS A VERB

LOVE
IS A VERB

by Mary Ellen Edmunds

Deseret Book Company
Salt Lake City, Utah

Library of Congress Cataloging-in-Publication Data

Edmunds, Mary Ellen, 1940–
    Love is a verb / Mary Ellen Edmunds,
        p.   cm.
    ISBN 0-87579-890-X
    1. Love—Religious aspects—Christianity. 2. Edmunds, Mary Ellen,
    1940–   . I. Title.
    BV4639.E34   1995
    248.4—dc20   94-24070
                                                  CIP

Printed in the United States of America

10 9 8 7 6 5 4 3 2 1

To Mom and Dad, who have done a lot more *show* than *tell*.
Love has always been a verb with them.

CONTENTS

PREFACE

With this little book I hope to awaken in you a remembrance of your own continuing adventures with love. It is the most gentle yet powerful force in the world, and our experience with it begins, if we are lucky, in our earliest childhood. I hope to stir some of those memories for you. I also hope that something in the book will be helpful to you in a specific way, lifting your spirits or comforting your heart or perhaps giving you an idea or two for making your neighborhood or your village or the world a better place.

Here they are, then, and I hope you enjoy them—my experiences with the Grasshopper Hospital, my sister Charlotte, the magic wand, carrot seeds, the Springville Post Office, my lost scriptures, the little girl in the pink shirt in a refugee camp in Thailand . . . memories of people and events that brought me closer to the realization that love really *is* a verb, and the joy comes from the *doing*.

My thanks go to the Deseret Book team for their help on this project. Many people went the second mile to help me in my first book–writing endeavor, and they made the journey seem like fun!

Some of the proceeds from the sale of this book are being donated to Enterprise Mentors, an organization founded in 1990 with the mission of helping people who live in developing areas to help themselves and each other. The effort is guided by the feeling that true compassion builds self–reliance and independence in the recipient; the emphasis is on individual initiative and personal responsibility. Thank you for helping.

Chapter 1

LOVE IS A VERB

I FIRST LEARNED ABOUT verbs from my third-grade teacher, Nellie Higbee. Verbs, she said, were action words like *kick*, *run*, *hit*, *jump*, *bite*, *scream*, and *fly*. The word *love* seemed more like a noun to me in those days. But gradually I began to realize that love is a verb as well. Love is doing. It's action.

Love without service, like faith without works, is dead.

You can serve without love, I suppose, but I don't think you can have genuine love without serving—you cannot feel compassion without feeling compelled to help in some way, to do what you can. Love is thus a powerful, peaceful force for good.

We all know the commandments telling us to "Love thy neighbor as thyself" and "Do unto others as you would have them do unto you." Remember, though, that a new commandment was given: The Savior taught that we should "Love one another *as I have loved you*." And He loves us constantly, patiently, and unconditionally. Maybe the commandment should be, "Do unto others as they want you to do unto them, as they need you to do, as Christ prompts you to do." Or it might even be, "Do unto others even if they never ever do unto you."

Many times, in many ways, our Heavenly Father gives us

1

specific opportunities to develop and practice that depth of love. We are allowed to share with each other, to serve each other, to develop more of the godliness that is within us— the mercy, the patience, the cheerfulness, the genuine kindness.

God invites us to serve those who are far away and those who are close, those we know and those we don't know— yet. He teaches us that we need each other. We're interdependent. No one knows it all or has it all. There are gaps and needs in each life, in each soul. We all reach out for help sometimes, when we encounter things we can't do or understand alone.

Pure love and service with compassion often involve sacrifice or, at the very least, inconvenience. People seldom begin relating a sweet story of extraordinary service with "It was on a day when I didn't have anything at all to do. I was just kind of 'hanging out.' I was about to call everyone I knew to see if they wanted me to do something." Usually such stories start out more like this: "It was a dark and stormy night," or, "I was so busy that day. I had a headache, the basement had just flooded, I forgot daylight saving time had started, my baby had swallowed a roll of film . . ."

We're usually cheerful about helping when we don't have anything else to do. But what if we *do* have something else to do? Something important. A marble tournament . . . or a TV show to watch . . . or what if I just got to bed . . . or I'm not in the mood . . . or it's for someone I don't like . . . or someone I don't know . . . or I have a test tomorrow . . . or if I wait three days, I can get credit for next month's visiting teaching assignment . . .

You're late for something? As some of my friends in other lands would say, "Don't be anxiety." It may be that you're late because someone needs you. Have you ever thought that someone somewhere may be pleading with Heavenly

Father for help and *you* may be the one chosen to help answer that prayer? The Good Samaritan may have been on his way to a prayer meeting or some other important appointment, but he was willing to stop and fill a need. If we're willing, God will use us.

Love requires courage. To share in Christ's way is a courageous undertaking. Do it. Do it now. Respond to promptings that come.

We must not ever ignore an impulse to serve when there's something we could do. When it's within our power to give love, we should never withhold it. If we feel compassion or empathy without doing something, we may diminish our power to act, to respond.

I find that I *think* of kind things more often than I *do* kind things. I'll get an idea, a prompting, but then too many times I chicken out. When I *do* respond, I have great adventures.

Once I was in a store standing in line to check out. (I have lots of experiences with that particular activity, and I almost always get in the slowest line; I don't know if it's a gift or a talent.) Anyway, I noticed that the woman behind the checkout counter seemed to be in a less-than-pleasant mood. She kind of locked horns with a person ahead of me in line. I couldn't really hear or tell exactly what happened, but the clerk was not happy. A little prompting came inside of me: "Say something nice to her." "I don't want to." "She needs it." (Do you ever have conversations like this with the still small voice?) "She'll bite my head off." Back and forth it went. I was getting closer. My heart was pounding the way it does when you sit in a testimony meeting and you know you're going to get up and you also know you're going to die at the pulpit.

And then I was there, right up close to her. She was punching the keys and all. And this is what came out of my mouth: "Are you having a bad day?" It came out kindly and gently and seemed to catch her way off guard. She looked at me, getting ready to bite, and then said, "Does it show?" "Kind of." She then told me that yes, she was having a very hard, bad, ugly day, and she told me some of the reasons why.

I didn't know what to do. I was screaming at the still small voice in my mind, "*Now* what? You didn't tell me what to do next!" But it came out: "Can I do anything to help you?" She looked at me with this what-in-the-world kind of look. It was an awkward moment. Then I said, "I know how to take out the trash." And we both laughed.

We continued talking to each other as she finished ringing up my purchases. She thanked me as I left, and I felt so happy I was grinning—not just smiling, but grinning. I felt good all over. I'm not sure if that little exchange did much for the woman at the checkout, but it made a huge difference in my day and is a sweet memory even now, years later.

Love as a verb is often spontaneous. It consists of things we think of on the spur of the moment, promptings to reach out and have the courage to be kind. It can be as simple as helping someone lift groceries into a car or picking up a little child who has fallen down. Let's not make spontaneous acts of love and kindness the exception to the rule. As my friend George Durrant says, "When it comes to giving, some people stop at nothing." I hope that will never be true of me.

Sometimes love is also by assignment. Visiting teachers or home teachers, Primary or Sunday School teachers, neighbors, big sisters or brothers—we can learn from everything we do to watch out for and show love to each other. As we find out by virtue of an assignment or some other relationship what's going on in homes and hearts, we'll have a better idea of what people need and want. That way we'll probably have a better idea of what we can do to make a difference.

We have many opportunities and assignments to offer our love in person, but some of the most interesting reactions occur when we share it anonymously. One night I returned home exhausted from a long shift at the hospital. My shift as evening nursing supervisor was to have ended around 11:30 P.M., but so much had happened and was still happening that I didn't get home until well after midnight. My white Clinic shoes weighed a hundred pounds each as I started up the stairs. And then I saw them: the flowers. A beautiful collection of colors wrapped in cellophane, waiting for me at the top of the stairs by my door.

It's hard to describe the happy feeling that came into my heart as I looked at the flowers and wondered why someone had given them to me. There was a little card with my name on the envelope. As I reached for it I was already thinking, "Oh, what can I do for them?" (As if we need to get even when someone does something kind for us.)

I got the flowers into my apartment and sat down to look at the card, wondering, "Who is it? Who did this kind thing for me?" The card said something like this: "Thank you, Mary Ellen, for being such a good friend. I appreciate your kindness and help. I love you." *And it wasn't signed!* Anonymous! Now what? How can you thank people if they don't tell you who they are?

Some interesting things happened to me. First, I went to bed thinking that someone loved me. Someone cared about me. Can we ever get too much of that? Second, I was going a little crazy. Who had done this? How could I say thanks and get it over with? Now I'd have to be nice to *everyone*— at least until the flowers died.

Finally, I began trying to decide who had done such a nice thing. Who would have given me such a wonderful

5

surprise? Interestingly, virtually everyone I knew and some I didn't know got onto my list of possibilities. Everyone in my family was on that list, and everyone at the hospital. When I arrived at work the next day and was making my rounds, I realized I was being very friendly, smiling a lot, greeting everyone with an extra effort to be genuinely interested. I'm sure some thought, "What's with Edmunds?"

As a result of that anonymous gift of love, I looked at everyone differently. Each person I saw might have been the one who had done such a nice thing for me. It was as if I took a new look at everyone I knew and found in them a kindness that I hadn't thought about or acknowledged nearly often enough.

As you think about your life, aren't the times that really stand out those when you've done things in the spirit of love? Not necessarily *big* things, right? More often it's the little things that make the real difference.

How about some low-tech love for those times when we don't have a lot of extra time, energy, money, food, ideas, clothing, or whatever. There are things anyone can do—even busy, busy worldlings. Don't wait for the big deal. Just serve here and now. Love is a lot of little rescues and burdens lifted and people genuinely served.

Give compliments. Find one, even if it's hard some days. "Uh, son . . . uh, I like the way you breathe! Yes! It's wonderful the way you breathe in and out, in and out, all the time! Faithfully! You're such a faithful son! So dependable in your breathing!"

Select someone you've been having a hard time with—a sister-in-law, a neighbor, whoever—and go to that person and make up. He or she will be so surprised. So happy. So amazed. So thankful. Say something like, "I set a goal not to talk to you for a whole year. I've now reached that goal, and I'm tired of being miserable. Can we talk?" Or how about this opener: "I've been appointed chairman of the Neighborhood Ash Wednesday celebration, and we wonder if you could please donate a pickle and two paper plates?" Find something *you'd* be comfortable saying or doing. But even if it's a little uncomfortable, mending a relationship is worth it.

Many gifts we give are little but make a big difference for someone—and for us too. One moment can make a difference in a whole hour or a whole day. I love the story of the woman at one of the busy tollbooths on a bridge near San Francisco who decided one morning to pay for herself and the ten cars behind her. Imagine! To be truthful, I can almost picture myself back in line thinking, "What's she doing? What's taking her so long? Why do I always get in such slow lines?"

Then I get up to the booth and the person in charge acts different than usual—more cheerful. And I receive the message: A woman who is long gone (so I can't thank her specifically) has paid my toll. Then I feel bad for being so impatient, and she has changed my day, and I even look for things I might be able to do that would have such a powerful effect on someone else.

Love doesn't need to cost something; it's not always a matter of money. The major components of love are an awareness and a willingness to act.

That awareness, that willingness, can take a lot of energy and a lot of work. And we have to remember that sometimes we can help and sometimes we just can't. We do the best we can. Some days are better than others. Some seasons of life provide more time and energy and other resources to help. If we all do what we can, according to what we have, to the extent of our ability in our particular season, it will be enough.

But we could love more if we sinned less, because sin

drains our batteries. Things like hate, jealousy, contention, and anger use up a lot of energy. The sweeter our relationship with God, the more we will long to serve and love Him and to make ourselves ready for anything He needs us to do. Maybe if we did some repenting, some returning to the Source of love, we would be able to discern promptings faster and better.

Another thing that runs down our love-and-service battery is trying to be a "topper" or a "bottomer." Sometimes moms do that without realizing it. You'd come home and say you'd had a hard day in junior high, and she'd say, "Well, when I was your age, I had to roller-skate fifty miles to baby-sit for five cents an hour." That's a bottomer.

And what's a topper? Someone says to you, "My son got an A on a chemistry paper," and you respond with, "Well, *my* son has been invited to open a yogurt shop on the moon." That's a topper. Neither a topper nor a bottomer be. It's too big a drain on your battery. If we could cut way down on competition and comparing, we'd have more time, energy, and love to share.

We'll have more time to love if we're not hooked on things that waste our time or strength or keep our hearts and minds unwisely occupied. Television, books, magazines, money (spending it or making it), entertainment, and many other things will take up all the time and energy we will give them. We can work to spend less time, energy, money, and other resources on things we don't really need, things that don't give us a good return on the investment.

Many of us want to help but suffer from serv-o-phobia: a fear of serving. We wonder what people will think or say. "Should I or shouldn't I?" we agonize within ourselves. If we will listen, we will hear that sweet answer, "Yes. Go ahead." And when the happy, peaceful feelings come, we wonder why we ever hesitated.

Not everyone will respond to our love in the way we would choose, of course. Sometimes when I get a less-than-positive response to something kind I've tried to say or do, I find myself thinking, "Later today when they look back on this they'll realize I was only trying to help. Then they'll smile and say, 'That was really nice.'" Anyway, if we give love to someone who does not seem to deserve or appreciate it, God will not be mad at us. Let's let Him be the judge—we can just love everyone.

If you have children, include them in your efforts to serve. Let them participate with you and learn firsthand the joys of performing meaningful service. Let them experience love in action. Remember the night from your childhood when your family put some bags of groceries on the front porch of someone in desperate need? You chose the fastest runner in the family to knock on the door and then join the rest of you in hiding down the block a bit. Remember how you felt when someone in that needy family came to the door and burst into tears and called everyone else to come and see? It's a blessed family that provides memories like that for the children.

Love is not only your sacks of groceries, your words, your clothing, your time, your loaf of bread—it's *you*. You have no idea how often you may rescue someone just by your countenance, the love that shines from your eyes. Maybe people can come close to you and feel safe—you provide a refuge.

In this world there is too much loneliness and sorrow. There are too many people who are overwhelmed and discouraged. There are too many terribly heavy burdens and tears and unanswered whys. But in this world of friends and neighbors and fellowcitizens, there is plenty of love for you and me and all of us. And there is enough joy for all the world, enough laughter and optimism and hugs and time and listening and reaching out. There's enough hope to give us a perfect brightness of hope, because we have a Savior and Redeemer. Jesus Christ is real. He lives. He will help us have enough time and energy for all He prompts us to do as we make *love* a verb. He loves us as we are and shows us how we can come to love as He loves.

If we could really figure out how to love, we wouldn't need a whole lot of other commandments. Not only would we reach out as we were able, but we in turn would receive help and comfort and the lightening of a burden when we needed it. Imagine—we would fill the world with love, until finally there simply wasn't room for unkindness, hate, contention, anger, impatience, envy, and other things that make us sick and sad. No one would be hungry or thirsty, physically or spiritually, for lack of attention and care. Wouldn't that be worth giving our time and our lives to?

I have come to know that the gospel of Jesus Christ is full of verbs, all related to the word *love*, verbs such as *feed, hug, mourn, serve, forgive, lift, succor, comfort, share, visit* . . . If we make *love* a verb, then *peace* becomes a noun, and *Zion* can be a reality. Let's allow love and service with compassion to become our need, our want, and our source of joy.

Chapter 2

LOVE AT HOME

THE THOUGHT OCCURRED to me sometime before I became a Beehive girl that I'd been spending a lot of time with the Edmunds family at 218 South First West. And I wondered *why*. Sometimes I would climb a tree and get in a comfortable position before facing questions this important and huge. Why was I a member of my family and not another? When I went to neighbors' homes they usually seemed happy to see me and treated me very kindly. That certainly wasn't always true in my own home with my own family. Why couldn't I just switch to the Palmers when things got rough? Just make a trade from 218 to 259—no big deal. Why didn't I live in a family who had a horse or bigger trees? Why not a family where I was the only child?

Why did I have to share a room and clothes and toys with Charlotte, my younger sister? Why did she have to go *everywhere* with me—to birthday parties and school activities, parades and vacations, swimming and sledding? Why did we always have to take turns at things, like going with Dad on a house call or practicing the piano or doing the dishes? Okay, I admit that on some things I would rather not have had a turn at all, but it all seemed to be part of this family thing.

Charlotte and I spent many nights wondering why our

older brother, Paul, had been put in our family. It was one of few issues that found us on the same side. It seemed to us that his main purpose in life was either to torment us or to get us into trouble.

As exasperating as he could be, though, I always wanted desperately to play with Paul and his friends. They had lots more fun than the girls in the neighborhood did. The unwritten but obvious rule was that if they let me play I couldn't act like a *girl*. Whether I was crawling into the caves that the Lombardi brothers were digging out behind the hospital (which of course would one day reach China) or helping to light firecrackers in anthills, I had to be brave and not act like a *girl*, or I couldn't keep playing with them.

Once when Mom and Dad were leaving for the evening, the last thing they said to me was something like, "And Mary Ellen, don't get on the garage!" I loved getting up on the roofs of things to see how far I could go in the neighborhood without touching land. Anything was fair game—garages, trees, sheds, chicken coops, homes, fences—just so I didn't touch the ground.

That particular night Paul and his friends were going to play chase, and oh, how I wanted to play. As usual, they said I could, *if* . . . and of course that meant "if you don't act like a girl." I promised I would play hard.

At one point Paul was "it" and he was chasing me. I climbed a tree that was right by the garage. Paul was right after me. There was no alternative—I *had* to jump onto the garage to keep from being caught by Paul. But of course then *he* jumped on the garage right after me. This garage didn't have a flat roof; the sides were pretty steep. It took skill and amazing balance to keep your footing. I'd had years of practice, even though I was only twelve, and I was good, but Paul was bigger and older and faster, and he was "it." I had no choice: I had to jump off the garage. The landing was not pretty. I knew immediately that something in my right ankle had gone very wrong.

Oh, it was awful! I wanted to scream and cry—but I wanted even more to retain my privileged, "not like a girl" standing. Paul jumped after me and tagged me, but he could tell that I wasn't up to being "it" right at the moment. I was a very wounded "it." Someone would have to be a proxy "it." Paul didn't seem to know what to do, so he just left me on the battlefield and ran after other players. Somehow I dragged myself into the house, through the sunporch, through the dining room, and into the living room where I got behind the couch and then let it all out. I sobbed in pain. I couldn't stand it any longer. I didn't care if I *was* a girl, I was a terribly wounded chase player, likely to die any moment. I cried as hard as I could.

And then Paul came in. He was very concerned. He took a look at my ankle and realized something was wrong; I could tell he felt bad about it. He said he knew what to do. He got a bucket, filled it with hot water, and stuck my ankle into it. The ankle ballooned before our eyes; I thought (and felt like) it was going to explode! We both realized that wasn't the best course of action, Paul's scouting experience notwithstanding, so he took my foot out of the bucket and called Dr. Farnsworth, our neighbor who was one of Dad's partners at the office. He came right away, took one look, and said my ankle was broken. Oh, the pain and agony! He suggested that Paul get some ice to put on it, which he did, trying not to hurt me.

And then we waited for Mom and Dad to come home. Paul kept assuring me that I was going to live and everything would be all right. He even told his friends he was through playing for that night, and they went home. It was kind of late when Mom and Dad came home, and I admitted right away that I'd been on the garage. I didn't want that

13

to come out later from Paul or Charlotte. I wanted to be the one to confess, right in the beginning—face up to the truth.

I kept watching to see what kind of reaction Mom and Dad would have to my disobedience. They were disappointed, but they weren't mad. Amazing! They seemed sorry that I was hurting so much. Dad asked me to try to stand on my ankle, and I can still remember the extreme pain I felt as I tried to do so. There was no way. He agreed with Dr. Farnsworth that I had probably broken my ankle and would have to have a cast put on the next morning. I don't remember how I made it through that Saturday night.

I do remember that the next day was Father's Day, and my father and I celebrated part of it together, just the two of us, at his office on Main Street. It was quite literally a bonding experience. He took an X-ray—sure enough, my ankle was broken. He put a cast on, with me helping a little bit here and there as I could. I remember watching his hands, glad that he knew what to do as he wrapped the plaster stuff around and around in just the right way. I remember how amazed and grateful I was that instead of being angry and trying to punish me, he was helping me to heal.

My ankle healed eventually. The memories remain: of Paul's tenderness and attention to me when I needed him, and of my parents' patience and willingness to let me say I was sorry and let it go at that. And in some small way I was receiving the answers to some of my wonderings: Maybe we were put into families to give us the chance to learn about the love of our Heavenly Parents through the love we receive from earthly parents. Maybe instead of getting angry and punishing us when we willfully break the commandments, Heavenly Father and Jesus do all They can to help us heal. Maybe on occasion a big brother can teach us a little about the role of and our need for our Elder Brother.

I had many opportunities to learn about my parents'

unconditional love for me. One such chance came in the 1950s when we got the first Volkswagen microbus in our town. It was fantastic! The front was flat, so you could pull it up right behind the car ahead of you and scare the heck out of people. The very first day we got it, Paul decided to drive it over to visit Larry a couple of blocks away and asked if I wanted to come. Sure! I loved the feeling, the smell, sitting up a little higher than usual, and having people look as we drove by.

Paul pulled up in front of Larry's house and said, "Why don't you take it for a spin around the block while I'm talking to Larry?" Now, I was only sixteen and had barely received my driver's license, so my first reaction was, Absolutely no way. I froze. It wasn't that I didn't want to, but I hadn't had a whole lot of driving experience and had never driven anything like this VW bus. It was tempting, though. "Just go around the block and come right back," Paul said, holding out the keys. He never did say "chicken," but perhaps I was thinking that. So I agreed. He headed up to Larry's front porch, and I got the bus into first gear and slowly rolled up the street. I think I may have gone to second gear, but not beyond that. I got to the corner and turned right—slowly, slowly. What a thrill! I turned right again. Everything was okay.

And then it happened. The sound, the terror, the shock, the disbelief! I miscalculated the clearance necessary and took out the door of our dentist's pickup truck, ruining the whole passenger side of our brand-new VW microbus! It *couldn't* be true! Oh, why had I said yes to going around the block? Why had the dentist parked his pickup truck in my way? *Why?*

Mom, of course, wasn't too thrilled to hear the news, and she told me to wait in my room until Dad got home from his office. I was as upset as I'd ever been in my life to that point.

It seemed like a very long afternoon, but eventually I heard Dad come home. I could hardly bear the pain of anticipation. I'd gone over and over all the possibilities in my mind as I waited in the bedroom.

Mom called me down to talk to Dad. He was sitting in the living room near the fireplace in the big red chair. I walked in feeling absolutely terrible but wanting to get it over with. As I remember it, I went over to him, knelt down by the chair, and started bawling immediately as I sobbed out my tragic story.

I wish I had a video of what happened next; I'd like to be able to remember it in much more detail. It went something like this: My father took me in his arms and told me it would be all right. He told me he knew I didn't mean to wreck the bus, and that he already had insurance, so we could get it fixed up. He said he was so thankful that *I* wasn't hurt (and he made sure that was true—that I wasn't hurt other than "internally").

Oh, the wonder of it! I cried so hard for relief—much harder than I'd cried out of fear and terror. I am convinced that I have learned more than I can accurately measure about Heavenly Father's ability to show *unconditional love* for me, and to freely forgive me, from my parents and my brothers and sisters.

Some of the best lessons came from sharing "everything" with Charlotte. I love this wonderful younger sister of mine more than I can say, but I didn't always know it or act like it. It took some time for me to realize how much I loved and needed her and how much it meant to me that she was always there for me. I guess I pick on her more than on my other sisters and brothers because we are closest in age and grew up doing so many things together with our very different personalities and styles.

The galling thing was, I mostly thought of her as being

perfect, never doing anything wrong, and it bugged the heck out of me. I got lots more spankings than Charlotte did—and I deserved them. I know that now, and I knew that then, but it didn't make it pleasant. You see, we really were different, this sister Charlotte and I. If she was a princess, then I was the wicked witch of the west. If she was a carrot, then I was a rutabaga. If she was a rose, then I was a weed—a noxious weed. I was the one who tested everything, and she was the one who would say, "Don't you just *love* the commandments? Don't you wish we had *more?*" Oh my.

One of the wonders of my upbringing is that our parents allowed us children—each of the eight of us—to be who we were, even encouraging us in our diversity, in our pursuit of the unusual. They let us learn by our experience and didn't always step in to interrupt consequences. Over and over again they let us work out our differences ourselves, even when we ran to them to help us with our "revenge." (Who was the first parent who thought of having two quarreling children wash windows facing each other?) I now feel grateful for having learned all the lessons I did through being so close to Charlotte. But the road was not always an easy one.

Lots of the problems we had happened at night. Charlotte and I shared a bedroom until we went away to college, and often after we'd been sent to bed but before we fell asleep I would get ideas. Then I'd have Charlotte carry out my dangerous plans. How did Mom and Dad always seem to know that I was the one who'd thought up the schemes?

I remember one night when all I wanted Charlotte to do was to jump out our second-story bedroom window and bend her legs just as she landed on the ground below, checking out a theory I had (based on what I'd seen in the Saturday matinee) that if she bent her legs on impact they wouldn't break. We were kind of going back and forth on this experiment—she didn't want to be the jumper, so she was making some noise, and I suppose I was too. We had received two warnings from Mom, but that was no big deal; she never came down the hall on Warning #1 or Warning #2. But then came Warning #3, and we knew her arrival was imminent. She was on her way , and she was *not* coming to tell us our allowance had been increased. Oh what to do, what to do. I suggested in a frantic whisper, "Hey, Charlotte! Let's see if we can fool Mommy. Let's trade beds!" She agreed. We traded—just in the nick of time.

I was hoping hard that Charlotte and I looked enough alike. Sure enough, Mom came in, went right over to Charlotte on *my* side of the room, flipped her over and spanked her, and walked back out with the typical, "Now you girls go to sleep!" Charlotte was crying, but I whispered in joy and amazement, "Charlotte! We did it. We did it! We fooled Mommy!" She was as proud as I was even though she was sobbing. What a brave and wonderful sister! She never did try that jump out our bedroom window.

How is it that through the years and experiences Charlotte could give me another chance, and another, and more and more? How could she be so forgiving? How is it that she believed in me over and over, even when I got her in so much hot water?

It's amazing—and touching—to me that the time I made big plans to run away from home, Charlotte didn't want me to go. I was off to California because my parents wouldn't get me a horse; I figured I'd try my luck with Uncle Joe or Uncle Chuck. After all the rotten things I'd done to Charlotte, she wasn't excited that I was leaving even though it meant she could have her own room. It didn't pan out anyway; I hadn't dragged my wagon full of hoarded cinnamon rolls and funny books very far in the summer heat before I was found by my friend Betsy's parents and accepted their offer of a ride home. I'm not sure Mom saw me returning—I had them let me out a little ways up the street—but I was welcomed back warmly. No fatted calf was killed and no celebration was held, but I knew I was part of that home and that family. I was accepted. Maybe we were put in families for our journey through this life because we can't run away, really—we stay and sort things out and learn some of our biggest, hardest, best lessons about unconditional love: theirs for us, and ours for them.

I still wanted a horse, but when it was clear that it was not going to materialize, I turned my thoughts to something else—something close at hand—that I could ride. Uncle Wilford kept a few sheep in a small pen out behind his house, and I started thinking that maybe we could ride them. It was worth a try. We had access to the pens from the back lots, so the idea was that we would go up the back lots, get in the pen, and have fun. We would do this *only* when Uncle Wilford's car wasn't there.

Oh, what fun! We had several sheep rodeos in the pen with happy, encouraging outcomes. Then, late one afternoon when we were having the time of our life, Uncle Wilford drove into the driveway and saw us. Stark terror! To make matters worse, at the very moment when Uncle Wilford drove in, one of the sheep jumped the fence. Oh no! A rodeo gone awry! Uncle Wilford had seen us, I knew, but he had his hands full trying to catch that sheep. We had to make an immediate escape. Abort the rodeo! Scatter! *Run for your life!*

The next day I saw Uncle Wilford walking down the street to our house, and I was convinced he was coming to tell my parents that he had contacted the police. But nothing happened. I couldn't believe it! I didn't go to prison or anything. It was a narrow escape, but it was a *real* escape. What did Uncle Wilford and my mom and dad talk about?

Did they decide I had learned a lesson without further pub-lic punishment? Did Uncle Wilford understand us the way Mom and Dad seemed to? Were most adults actually willing to be patient and forgiving? Were they thinking of their own childhood and perhaps laughing at our experiences? Maybe we need more Uncle Wilfords in the world of chil-dren growing up.

It so happened that we moved from our hometown, something we never thought would happen, when I was sev-enteen and Charlotte fifteen. It was a hard adjustment, but in a way it was wonderful. We suddenly realized that we no longer had any friends—we had left behind everyone and everything familiar except for *us*. Our family. That was when Charlotte and I quit scratching, hitting, punching, and arguing so much and became best friends. There's no one—*no one*—like your very own sister. We went on to become nurses, Charlotte at Ricks for two years and me at BYU for four years. We graduated within a couple of weeks of each other and had the chance to be roommates and to work together at the hospital in Provo. There's no way to express adequately what it means to me to have a best friend who is also my sister.

And who would have guessed that Paul, the big brother who did his best to scare the heck out of us when he tended us, who acted as if he didn't even like us, whose every energy seemed bent on making our lives miserable, would end up loving us the way he did. He and I both worked at Zion National Park one year, and he always made sure to warn me about raids on the girls' dorm, slipped me an extra "just-in-case" five dollars from time to time, and took care to see that I was all right.

Thank goodness for families and for home, for a chance to learn some of life's hardest but most important lessons in a safe place. My heart aches for children who are born in situations where there is no safety and little unconditional love. Thank goodness for parents who have learned how to allow their children to become who they are. I look at the eight of us now, all living relatively close to each other, and I rejoice in our friendship and our unconditional love for each other as we continue to grow. All of my brothers and sisters have children, and I watch the cycle continue as those children go through similar lessons and opportunities. Thank goodness for the chance to experience life and learn the big and little lessons of relationships, choices, and what it means to head for Home with the kind help of those closest to us.

Chapter 3

CARROTS

CARROT SEEDS DON'T LOOK at all like carrots. They look to me like little specks of dirt. They're not orange. They're not shaped like carrots. You couldn't take them to a picnic. Well, I guess you could, but there's no way to make carrot sticks out of them, and those little seeds can sure get stuck in your teeth. I've tried eating carrots that way. Not satisfying. Those little specks aren't full of vitamins and good stuff yet.

I look at those little seeds and wonder, How do they *know?* How do they know they're carrots and not squash or apple trees or petunias or some exotic, noxious weed? To me it is a miracle that this tiny, dirtlike speck is a carrot, sitting in that little package and waiting for someone to help the next step happen.

The next step is for someone who has faith that a carrot is waiting in that little, tiny, non-orange, non-carrot-shaped seed to plant it and then to provide the water and sunshine and time, the weeding and waiting. And what do you know! Eventually little green tops begin to appear, and a carrot is forming in the ground, the seed having broken apart to allow a miraculous process to take place.

Personally, I've always been somewhat nervous about planting carrot seeds. There's no arrow on the seeds: "This side down" or "This side up." What if I were to plant them upside down? People would drive through the neighborhood pointing and laughing. "Ha! Look at Edmunds! She planted her carrot seeds upside down! The orange is coming out of the ground first!" Even this, then, is a miracle—how does it happen that the orange goes down and the green comes up out of the ground to help provide nourishment and growth to the orange? All this is beyond my comprehension.

And there's another thing. The seeds look alike. They really do. They're tiny, but if you look at them closely, you see that they're pretty much the same size, shape, and color. And yet even in the pictures on packages of seeds, where they've lined up a few of the best carrots they can find for a family photo, those carrots are just not exactly the same. Each one is unique—different from every other carrot.

You might try this (I did, and I must warn you that I've lost my privileges at a certain grocery store): Go to the produce section at the store and find where the carrots with the green tops still on them are stacked up, waiting for someone to come who needs them for a dinner or a picnic. There they are, looking very nice. Put all of them on the floor, spread them out, and try to match up the ones that are identical twins.

You know, don't you, even as you read this, that you won't find any two that are exactly alike. That's not the way it happens. Even when they're tiny seeds, carrots know they're unique. Somehow they know.

Now of course, if I keep the seeds in the package (which I've done with a few hundred of them, and I feel bad about it, except that it helps me to make this point from time to time), they'll never become carrots. They've got to be planted. They've got to be given a chance to release the power that is in them, and there are certain conditions that have to be met for that to happen. I can't just put them on the sidewalk, or in a drawer, or even on top of pretty good dirt, and say, "Go to it!" They need to be planted. They need to have water and sunshine and time and care. And oh—the miracle as the green comes up and the orange goes down and another unique carrot is born!

Maybe people are like that—waiting for the miracle that will help them become who they are. My sister Charlotte and I used to work together in the nursery at the hospital, and we were convinced that each baby was absolutely unique. Sometimes we even gave them code names, especially the newborns who stayed for a few days or weeks. They seemed to have arrived with personalities and unique characteristics already in place.

It is a sobering and tender experience to look at a newborn baby and wonder about who he or she is. Do those children know who they are? Do their parents know? Maybe they're like little seeds, with the potential in them to become unique, special, wonderful children of God.

Some of the same questions we asked about carrots come into this wondering about children. How do they know? How do they know they're Charlotte and not Mary Ellen? Frank and not John? What kind of care is needed for the miracle to happen? How do we "plant" a person? How do we help provide the sunshine and water, the weeding and care and time? We can't just put the baby on the sidewalk or in a drawer and expect that something miraculous will happen.

Yet here they are, millions born every day, and their potential is part of their heritage: Each one is a child of God. Their Heavenly Father is a King. They are born with the potential to become as He is! Pondering that is even more wonderful than looking at a tiny carrot seed and being awed that the little speck can become an orange carrot with a green top.

And yes, each little baby is definitely different from all

the rest. Even those born into the same family, with the same parents, who eat all the same things for breakfast and lunch as the years go by, and hear the same stories and music, and ride in the same car or bus, and play with the same toys—they still turn out different. When we sing a phrase like "You're not a clone" we really mean it—no two are exactly alike. Each comes with a unique soul and perhaps with a unique mission and purpose. Maybe each little person-seed might even need special, unique care to reach its full potential, to become perfect: whole, complete, and pure. Finished. Godly.

Author Timothy Gallwey draws a similar analogy: "When we plant a rose seed in the earth, we notice that it is small, but we do not criticize it as 'rootless and stemless.' We treat it as a seed, giving it the water and nourishment required of a seed. When it first shoots up out of the earth, we don't condemn it as immature and underdeveloped; nor do we criticize the buds for not being open when they appear. We stand in wonder at the process taking place and give the plant the care it needs at each stage of its development. The rose is a rose from the time it is a seed to the time it dies. Within it, at all times, it contains its whole potential. . . . At each stage, at each moment, it is perfectly all right as it is" (*The Inner Game of Tennis* [New York: Bantam Books, 1974], 29).

Roses and carrots and people. They don't look (or behave) up to their potential in all circumstances, in all stages of their growth and development, but they always have the power in them to become, especially if careful attention is given to helping this process happen. And I do feel that it is a process, this becoming who or what we really are.

President Gordon B. Hinckley said something that seems to me to apply: "We are far from being a perfect society as we travel along the road to immortality and eternal life. The great work of the Church in furthering this process is to help men and women move toward the perfection exemplified by the Savior of mankind. We are not likely to reach that goal in a day or a year or a lifetime. But as we strive in this direction, we shall become better men and women, sons and daughters of God" (*Church News*, 6 Mar. 1982). That thought helps me to remember that perfection is a process, and we need to continue to strive to be who we really are: more like our Heavenly Father, more like our Savior and Brother.

When I was first called as a missionary, people told me I was going to a place where everyone looked the same. Having not had much experience in my life up to that point, I didn't know what they meant. Then, in August of 1962, I arrived in Hong Kong. Wow! Because I lacked experience, all the people did look alike to me.

I found myself wondering, "How do they know they're them?" (not worrying at all about the grammar in such a question). They looked so much alike that I wondered, "How do they know if it's their children coming home for dinner?" I could almost picture a wife asking, "Are these ours?" and the husband responding, "I'm not sure." She: "How many are there?" He: "Six." She: "Well, we have six. Let's feed them. They might be ours."

Then people began to have names. Mickey Chang. President Hu. Sister Lin. And I looked back and laughed at myself for ever thinking that they looked alike. Each was so wonderfully individual. How could I ever have thought all the people looked alike, any more than I could go to a market and think all the carrots were exactly alike? I loved getting to know and love and appreciate my friends in Asia one by one. In fact, when I returned home it seemed that people here reminded me of people there.

While I was serving in the Philippines as a health missionary, my companion and I went about once a month to the city of Baguio, an eight-hour bus ride from Manila. There we taught lessons to the members of the branch and helped in any way that was needed. Each time we got to the bus station in Baguio, a certain little girl would meet the bus. We got to be buddies even though we didn't speak each other's languages. She knew very little English beyond "Hey, Joe. Where are you going, Joe?" And we didn't know much Tagalog. Still we communicated and became friends. She was there each time, selling her peanuts and newspapers.

On one of our visits I took a picture of that little girl. She looked with some interest and curiosity at my camera. I remember thinking that perhaps she hadn't seen too many of these "aim-and-shoot" varieties. We took the film back to Manila and got it developed. On our next trip to Baguio we had a picture to give her—a picture of herself, there at the bus station with her peanuts and papers.

I guess it's not uncommon to have something go through your mind before it actually happens. I do that quite a lot—think ahead of things I might say and even of things people might say back to me. As we approached Baguio I had it in my mind that we'd get off the bus, hug our little friend as usual, and then I'd give her the picture. She'd smile and squeal and say something about not having many pictures of herself, and thank you very much, things like that.

We arrived, and there was our little friend. We hugged each other and exchanged enthusiastic greetings as usual. Then I handed her the picture. She took it and looked intently. Then she looked up and asked, "Sino?" ("Who's this?") That hit me right in the heart. It had not even crossed my mind that she wouldn't know what she looked like—that she wouldn't recognize a picture of herself.

I admit that sometimes when I see myself in a mirror I'm

caught off guard—frightened or something. But I know what I look like. I can recognize myself. Here was a little child who didn't know who she was, even what she looked like. It made the tears come. I responded, "Ikau." ("It's you.") "Ako?" ("It's me?") "Yes." So she looked harder at the picture but still couldn't seem to realize that it was a picture of her.

Then I got an idea. She always had on the same shirt, and it had a hole in it. I pointed to the hole and made a kind of "see this?" look on my face. She nodded. I then pointed to the hole in her shirt in the picture. Again, "See this?" She did. I touched her face and then her face in the picture. "It's you." And then her little countenance changed. She understood. "Ako! Ako!" ("It's me! It's me!")

How does Heavenly Father help us to know who we are, to be able to shout with joy, "It's me! It's me!" I think He gives us a variety of experiences that help us to know more about our real selves. He shows us to ourselves in many interesting ways.

Several years ago my parents celebrated their fiftieth wedding anniversary. We kids didn't know if they would make it that long or that far—we thought we might wear them out. The eight of us are so active and so different. But they did it. As part of the celebration they put their vast collection of old 16mm home movies on video. In about 1937, before they were married, someone gave them a 16mm movie camera, the kind that looks like a black box. Dad wound it up and "shot us" many times over those fifty years.

So as we gathered for the anniversary celebration we sat together in the living room to watch the videos of the perfect family growing up. Oh yes. So perfect. Here we are going to church, scriptures in hand, thrilled to wear our Sunday clothes and be reverent for quite a while. (No way.) Here we are starting out on a vacation, and I'm saying, "Oh no, Mommy, I don't want to sit by the window. It's Charlotte's turn. No, I had a turn last time. I love Charlotte. I want her to sit by the window." (Ha. Fat chance. I was probably actually screaming, "She touched me!" or something like that.)

It's all there on the films—samples of our hopefully normal growing up together. Paul K. Jr., Mary Ellen, Charlotte Norine, Susan, Franklin Middleton, John M., Ann M., and Richard M. (all the M's for Middleton, my mother's maiden name). It's quite a feeling to see yourself at a point where you can no longer remember having been. But there you are. You know it's you by the pictures and because Mom and Dad point you out and say how cute and clever you were. "That's you, Mary Ellen—you were always bending over and putting your head between your legs!" I can't do that anymore.

Well, I got to thinking about all of this. Did Heavenly Father take movies of us? Are there videos of what we were like and who we really are? Will we see those heavenly home movies one day? Will we have that wonderful feeling of knowing that we did all we could to find the real us inside all our lessons and experiences?

Part of what helps us know who we are is how others treat us. We're asked to esteem our brothers and sisters as ourselves—to be *one*. The invitation seems to refer not only to those who are like us but to all who come within our sphere, our influence. In other words, carrots need to be kind to turnips and not look down on them just because they're not carrots.

I have in my possession a record that I won as a prize in a fifth-grade art contest. It's pretty much scratched to death by now, but I still have it. It's called "The Churkendoose," and it tells the story of an egg that everyone took turns sitting on—the chicken, turkey, duck, and goose. And so when the baby thing hatched it was a combo—part chicken, part turkey, part duck, and part goose—a Churkendoose.

Because this Churkendoose was a strange and different kind of beast, others made fun of it. It got very lonely. It sang some songs about how it felt, how painful it was not to be treated kindly: "Does the pear tree say to the apple tree, 'I hate you 'cuz you're not like me'?" In the end the Churkendoose saved the others from a fox—chased it away—and then everyone was nice to him.

Sometimes I've felt like a Churkendoose—looking different because of my braces or feeling left out at a party or whatever. All my life I've been grateful for friends who have treated me kindly and helped me through my awkwardness.

Once a group of Relief Society presidents in a training session were asked to think of the names of as many young women in their ward as they could. Not "Ethel's daughter" or "the Mason girl," but the girls' front names, their very own names. Some of the presidents expressed embarrassment that they didn't know very many names. We are asked to pay attention to each other and not just to those who are like us in age, in experience, or in any other category that might isolate us from others. Do you know the names of the Sunbeams and deacons and Beehive girls in your ward? Do you know something about them?

Years ago I heard a story about a large family that went on a vacation. Mostly they bought food in grocery stores and ate in parks to save money, but once in a while they went into a restaurant. They always caused quite a stir, as there were so many of them. Tables and chairs generally had to be rearranged to accommodate them.

On one such adventure they finally got seated and the waitress was taking their orders. She took a few orders and then got to a little boy around eleven years old. "And what would you like?" she asked. He looked over at his mother. After all, she usually chose for him. It was an awkward moment, but the mother didn't say anything, so he looked at the waitress and said, "I'll have a hot dog!"

At that moment his mother regained her voice and said, "Oh, no, he'll have what the rest of us are having." The waitress didn't seem to hear that comment and continued looking at the little boy. "What would you like on the hot dog?" He squirmed a bit and looked again at his mother. She once again seemed to lose her voice. So the little boy excitedly told the waitress what he wanted on the hot dog: mustard, pickles, onions, ketchup. She wrote it down, took the rest of the orders, and left.

The little boy was amazed. He couldn't believe it. He turned to everyone else at the table and said, "She thinks I'm real!"

Is there someone in your life whom you treat as real who needs that more than you may realize? Is it someone older? Younger? Taller? Shorter? A longer carrot? A different-colored rose? Oh, if we could only enjoy our diversity, our differences! It seems that God must have made us different on purpose. Is it so we can find help for our needs? Is it so we can find others who need us? Is it so we need to team up with others to find our wholeness and completeness?

Carrot seeds are all around us waiting to be planted or watered or weeded or tended in some other important way. May we watch over and care for each other, helping the miracle of our uniqueness to happen.

Chapter 4

INSTRUMENTS

ONE DAY MANY YEARS AGO a friend and I were driving in the Avenues in Salt Lake City on our way somewhere when we noticed a young mother standing out by her truck looking very frustrated and unhappy. We were prompted to stop, and we did so. The woman had several children watching and waiting. She had run out of gas on her way to pick up a daughter from a dancing lesson and couldn't believe her bad luck. We said we'd go get some gas for her. Although she was grateful for the help, she also seemed to feel uncomfortable being on the receiving end. But what could she do?

We drove till we found a gas station, pumped a couple of gallons into a borrowed container, and then returned to the woman and put the gas in the truck. The woman was thankful but still a little embarrassed to accept our help. She wanted to know how much she owed us. We told her that it just so happened that the gas station was having a super deal that day and the one-hundredth customer would receive two gallons of gas free and we just happened to be the hundredth customer. Can you imagine, she doubted that was true! We've probably all felt what she was feeling—that awkward moment when we're not quite sure how to say thank you, and we think we'd feel better if we could pay for kindness.

Then an idea came to me, and I said to her, "You'd do the same for us." That stopped her—she thought about it, then broke into a smile, and said, "You're right. I would." All of us would, wouldn't we . . . if we just knew. We'd all say Yes! to the promptings that come to us if we weren't in such a hurry, or if we weren't so shy or so worried that we wouldn't know what to do or say if we offered to help.

One interesting thing about that experience is that I can't remember anything about where I was going that day, but I'll never forget the brief, eternal experience of helping someone—of heeding the prompting that she needed help and there was some little thing we could do that would make a big difference for her and for us. Was it planned? Were we directed to the spot where she was? Were we instruments?

The feeling that comes into our hearts and motivates us to say yes to the Spirit's promptings is compassion. I'm sure it's tied to love, to charity. I have always been convinced that when you're filled with compassion you have to do something. Some experiences I've had have felt like a hands-on seminar about taking action. That was the way it was that day in the Avenues, and it's been like that quite a few times in my life.

It's as if I'm being tested to see not only if I'll listen to the still small voice but if I'll respond—if I'll "just say yes." Not maybe, not no, not "I'm not in the mood to be an instrument right now," not "Get someone else," but "Yes! I'll do what I can. Please give me some good ideas. Please give me courage and energy. Here we go!"

There seem to be quite a few books on the market about how to say no, how to take care of yourself ("number one"). Some almost seem to teach us how to be separate and protected from other people. And we do have only so much energy, so much time, so many resources. But I have noticed that there are also some very important books on how to say yes, how to respond to and care for others in a Christlike way. There are more than 3,728 pages of examples and instructions in the scriptures.

There is no substitute for the scriptures and the Spirit in helping us strive to love and serve and become more like our Savior. They will teach us to be better instruments in His hands, more willing and more able to say yes.

I had an unforgettable experience a few years ago on a hot August evening. I stopped at the post office in Springville to get my mail. Mapleton, where I live, doesn't have a post office, and Springville's is the closest one. It's always after hours when I go there, so usually there's no one around. But that evening as I walked in I noticed a man standing at the automatic stamp dispenser looking frustrated. He looked as if he might have come from Mexico; many come from there to help us harvest our crops.

This man was trying to get the stamp machine to take his money and give him some stamps but was apparently having problems. I took all of this in as I turned and walked to my box. A strong, deep feeling came into my heart that I wanted to help the man get his stamps. And I had a distinct impression: "This is compassion you're feeling."

I got my mail, sorted it, and then walked over to the man. "Isn't it working, sir?" "No," he replied, looking at me helplessly. I had never used one of those machines, but I wanted so much to help that I said, "Let me try." I took his extremely worn five-dollar bill and tried to get the machine to take it. I tried several times. All kinds of approaches. It wouldn't work.

I handed the bill back to the man and mumbled something like, "It won't work." He looked back at me as if to say, "That's what I said." I said, "Hold on a sec." He obviously had no idea what I meant. I went to my car (thinking he probably thought I had left and wouldn't be back) and returned with my purse. I took out my three newest one-dollar bills and approached the machine.

The man was watching with what seemed to be a whole lot of curiosity. I put a dollar bill in, and the machine took it. I shouted, "Yippee!" The machine took the other two one-dollar bills, too, and with a sense of accomplishment and joy I said, "Sir! It's working!" We got a book of stamps and a dime for change. That was my first experience with such a machine, and I wanted the man to be as excited as I was.

This was happiness. I handed the book and the dime to the man and said, "Sir, we got it! Here you go!" He started shaking his head no. I said, "Yes—these are yours." He backed away a bit saying, "No, no—you don't do this . . . " I said, "Yes I do—I just did! These are your stamps."

He wouldn't take them. I didn't know what to do. Then I got an idea. I said the first thing that came into my mind on that very hot August day: "Merry Christmas, sir!" He had to smile. He couldn't help it. He took the stamps and the dime.

Then he looked at his worn five-dollar bill, and I sensed it was all he had. He asked hesitantly, with an accent, "How much I owe you?" I said, "Nothing. *Nada*." He seemed confused. "No," he said and tried to give the stamps back to me. I wouldn't take them, but I didn't want him to feel bad. So I said, "Sir, you would do the same for me." He kind of smiled at that and nodded yes, he would. I told him I knew that.

I walked out of the post office on Cloud 10. I felt so wonderful. It hit me: three minutes, three bucks—cheap! I treasured that genuine feeling of joy and shouted happily all the rest of the way home. It was the real thing, all natural ingredients. I'll never forget it.

Then I had another thought that added even more meaning to the experience. I imagined Them Up There somewhere in a meeting. Yes, in a meeting. (It's hard for me not to imagine Heavenly Father and those who work with Him having lots of meetings. After all, it's been said that the fourteenth article of faith is "We believe in meetings—all that have been scheduled, all that are now scheduled, and we believe that there will yet be scheduled many great and important meetings. We have endured many meetings and hope to be able to endure all meetings. Indeed we may say that if there *is* a meeting, or anything that resembles a meeting, or anything that we might possibly turn into a meeting, we seek after these things.")

So I pictured Them Up There in a meeting. I could imagine someone interrupting the meeting with an important message: "Excuse me. I hate to interrupt, but there's a man down there in the Springville Post Office, and he's trying to get some stamps and can't make the machine work."

Wouldn't it be something if someone in the meeting had said, "It's okay. Edmunds is on her way. She'll help him. We can go back to the agenda." Wouldn't it be a wonderful thing if God could count on MEE? (I've been an acronym all my life.) Wouldn't it be wonderful if we could just say Yes! when He invites us to participate in kindness?

Many have prayed for the chance to be instruments in God's hands. I had an unforgettable learning experience about that when I was a student nurse. I was about to witness my first "grand opening"—I was going to watch a surgeon perform an operation. I was all suited up: I had on the green gown and cap, the white mask, and the gloves, and my hands were pointed upward and in front of me. Don't touch anything that isn't sterile. Clean on clean, dirty on dirty.

I was getting warm. Very, very warm. I began to think I might faint and hit the floor and embarrass myself and my instructor and possibly do damage to my nose. So I said to myself, "Self, you've got to focus on something else. Think about something different." I looked around the room, fascinated by all that is involved in surgery. Then my eyes landed on the tray that was set up near the operating table. It had instruments on it. All the instruments looked shiny and new. Sparkling. Ready. And there were the scalpels, all sharp and poised.

The surgeon came in. He was a masked man, but I knew who he was, and I knew something about what he was going to do. I started worrying for the woman who was being wheeled into the room. Hey! This is going to hurt! Should I do something? Should I save her? This was real. Fortunately I decided that the surgeon and everyone else on the team had a desire to help and the knowledge and skill to do so. So I tried just to watch and not be worried about how much this was going to hurt.

They gave the woman some anesthetic and she went to sleep and the team went to work. The surgeon would hold his hand at his side, almost behind him, and ask for something. The nurse by the tray would snap it on his gloved hand so he knew he had it, and he'd work on without having to look around much. Soon it was time for the scalpel. It was snapped into his hand, and he made the incision on the woman's abdomen. (Ouch!)

The doctor continued working, going deeper and asking for different instruments. The scalpels came into the scene quite often, it seemed. And I began thinking about them. What if they had minds of their own? That scalpel he was using right then—what if it suddenly decided it didn't want to do what the surgeon was directing it to do, and it started just chopping around, exploring and slicing and . . . well, you get the idea.

And then the lesson began to come. Scalpels don't do that. They don't go off on their own. They're instruments in the hands of the surgeon, and he knows what he's doing. They're part of the team, but they do what they're directed to do. I thought about the perspective the surgeon had that the scalpel didn't—a perspective that no one else on the team had. That was why they had put that particular instrument in his hands. Amazing. He knew what he was doing.

It seemed to me at first that he was going to hurt the patient, but really he intended to help heal her. Maybe he was part of an even bigger team. Perhaps her family was praying for her. Maybe someone she loved and trusted had given her a blessing. There were likely lots of members of the team, lots of instruments in the hands of God, being led by His knowledge and perfect perspective and His wonderful, healing hands.

I want God to be able to use me as an instrument. I want Him to be able to count on me to do what I can to help.

One evening a couple of years ago I left work a little bit late. As I was going down 9th East I saw Matt, one of the fellows I work with, evidently waiting for the bus. So I pulled over, rolled down the window, and said, "Hey, sailor, can I give you a ride?" He laughed but hesitated, saying he lived quite a distance away. I said, "It's right on my way!" He said he knew it wasn't, but I insisted that I could go anywhere I wanted, and if it was on my way, it was on my way. So he got in, and off we went toward his home.

He lived in an apartment right across from a discount bakery place, which he pointed out. As I dropped him off I said I'd go over there and check it out. It was getting close to closing time, and there were only two or three cars in the parking lot. I parked a couple of spots away from one of them and glanced at it as I went in the store. Someone was just sitting in it—probably waiting for someone who'd gone in to do some shopping. I went into the store and wandered around looking at all the good stuff. Got a few loaves of bread, and when I came out I noticed that the car was still in the parking lot. A young woman and two children were sitting inside; I could tell they were having some trouble.

I decided to stop and see if I could help, but I would put my bread in my car first. As I walked past the car with the woman and the children, I was touched with a very strong feeling of compassion. I heard myself say something, but it was as if the words were put into my mind: "I will not leave you alone." It was a very strong, tender feeling. I smiled. I had intended to go over and see if I could help, but that feeling and those words let me know that Someone was watching out for that woman and wanted me to try to help.

I walked over to her and asked if she was having trouble. Yes—she couldn't seem to get her car started. I told her I had jumper cables, but I wasn't sure how to use them. I am not a genius with cars. I'm not an anything with cars besides just knowing how to get them started and how to steer. I asked her to try it again, but when she turned the key there wasn't any noise, so it didn't seem like jumper cables would have helped. I asked if I could call someone for her. Her husband was at work and couldn't be reached. She thought of the number of a neighbor, and I called there but got an answering machine.

She was frustrated, and I didn't know what to do, how to help. I said I would go look in the store for someone who looked nice and smart. A man in there with his wife and son was just checking out. I made myself brave and asked, "Do you know anything about cars?" He kind of shrugged and said he knew a little bit. I asked if he could come and

39

look at a car and see if he could help get it started. He looked at his wife, and she said she and the son would wait.

We went outside, and he looked under the hood. I held the hood up; the latch was broken, so I was the hood holder for the next part of the adventure. He fussed around and had the woman try to start the motor a few times. Meanwhile his wife and son got into their car to wait. I asked how far away he lived, and he said "Price," which was quite a way to go. I was worried that he was going to be late starting back to Price, but he kept trying to find solutions to the problem.

A man watching us from the other side of the fence around the store called out, "Do you need some tools?" The Price Man said he thought maybe that would help, so the Fence Man drove his truck and dog around and into the parking lot and got out a bunch of tools. An interesting character, with long, thinning, straggly hair, some of which was in a ponytail, and a long beard. And a can of beer. And a very kind heart. He propped up the hood with a ski pole, which took away one of my responsibilities. But I still held it anyway—afraid it would fall and kill them both.

The Fence Man got in and helped, and they did lots of stuff, including putting a hole in the radiator hose, which they then had to fix. Finally, after about an hour and a half, they had done what they could and asked her to try again. The car almost started . . . but didn't. I suggested she just lock it up, and I would take her home. I gave the Price Man some wipes for his hands. The Fence Man wore gloves. Both were kind, and we thanked them sincerely, and then they left.

The woman during all this time was trying to keep the kids quiet and calm. At some point she came around and stood near me, looked at me, and said, "You're Sister Edmunds, aren't you." It caught me off guard, because we'd

been there for quite a while by that time. I said, "Yes, I am."
Then she said, "I heard you speak at the MTC and at
Ricks." We talked about her experiences there a little bit.
And from that point on I was thinking, "What if I hadn't
helped? What if I had left her alone?" Probably she had
heard me share these great, glorious ideas about helping
each other and serving and doing things even if they're
inconvenient and blah blah blah. But would I practice, or
just preach?

It's exactly what I try so hard *not* to do—give talks but
not live what I say. I try to "walk my talk," as I've heard
some express it. So that got to me. It was a big lesson. That
woman knew who I was. She knew when I walked past her
into the store, and she knew when I came out and headed
for my car—and when I came back to try to help. I had
no idea that she knew. And I wasn't able to do much—I
couldn't get her car fixed—but I did what I could. I bundled
her, her two children, a car seat, and her purchases into my
car and took them home, not too many blocks away. I
helped her carry things in. She was grateful. I was, too, more
than I could adequately tell her or Heavenly Father. "I will
not leave you alone."

I want my Heavenly Father to see me near a bread store
or a post office or in a grocery store or walking down a street
and be able to whisper to me through the still small voice
that someone needs help and He needs an instrument. "Can
I borrow you for a few minutes?" I can almost hear Him say.
"Someone's having a problem, and I think your approach
will be just right for this adventure. What do you say?"
What can I say except yes? Although He has asked me to do
some very hard things, He's never ever asked me to do
something that He wouldn't help me accomplish.

And I've noticed another thing, something that's hard to
explain. It's like the feeling we get that nine pennies go

further than ten when we begin to realize that paying a full tithing and a generous fast offering can open the windows of heaven. For me it has turned out to be that way with time. Nine minutes go further than ten. The Lord won't ask me to help without making it up to me.

Now, certainly the post office isn't the only place where we can have wonderful experiences as instruments, but for some reason it has been such a place many times for me. One evening when I walked in I noticed a very pregnant woman standing near the change machine. She seemed frustrated. I started to smile as I walked toward my box. I knew something wonderful was about to happen.

I got my mail and then walked back over to her and asked, "Isn't it working?" She sighed and shook her head. "I tried so hard to get here before the post office closed," she said, "but I didn't make it. And now it says that the machine is out of change." I looked at the blinking sign and said, "Well, that seems weird, that they'd be out of change so soon after closing time. You'd think they'd check those things." Then I told her to wait a second, and I headed out to my car.

I returned with my purse, and we put all the coins we had together on the counter. Between us we had enough for her to get the stamps she needed. Then she tried to give me a dollar bill. I backed away in amazement, protesting, "I don't take money from strangers! Who do you think I am?" We both laughed. She said, "Well, tell me your name, then, so I can thank you." I said the first thing that came into my mind: "I'm Elsie the Borden Cow." I have no idea why I said that, but we both laughed again.

The woman thanked me and seemed to feel a little awkward, so I said, "You'd do the same thing for me." She laughed and seemed touched and responded with feeling, "Yes, I would." I said, "I knew that—didn't you know that?"

I started toward the door and she said, "Elsie?" I turned. "Yes?" "Whenever I come to the post office I'm going to see if there is anyone I can help." I smiled out loud. Yes! There's you, there's me, there's the man at the stamp machine and the woman at the discount bakery—we're all in this together! We all want to be instruments in God's hands. Oh, what a wonderful feeling.

Another time when I was in the post office (has this become one of my favorite places or what?) I was pulling the stuff out of my box and noticed one of those small cards with a picture of a child and the question, "Have you seen me?" I started thinking that I had thrown away thousands of those, but then I remembered that my parents have told me a million times not to exaggerate. But I *have* thrown away a whole bunch of those cards. I never knew anyone who was pictured on them. They'd never be in Mapleton anyway; they'd most likely be in a big city a long ways away.

On this particular day, though, something about the question grabbed my attention and touched my heart. "Have you seen me?" I didn't know the child on the card, although I wished I had seen her and could help her get home. But the question was broad enough to include all of Heavenly Father's children who might be feeling lonely and lost and far from home. "Have you seen me? I'm lost. I want to go home, and I don't know how. Can you help me?" Just say yes. Yes, I can help, and I will. I'll do what I can. Use me, Father in Heaven. Help me know what to say and how to say it. Help me know what to do and how to do it.

It occurs to me that we are never invited to participate in acts of kindness without the promise that we'll receive ideas to help in our response. It's as if with the invitation, the feeling of compassion, comes an increase in our ability to respond in a helpful, kind, Christlike way. We become more whole and complete ourselves as we reach out to lift and bless others, to comfort them and mourn with them, to do what we can to make their burdens bearable.

President Ezra Taft Benson taught that God can help us increase our abilities if we will just give ourselves to him. "Men and women who turn their lives over to God will find out that he can make a lot more out of their lives than they can. He will deepen their joys, expand their vision, quicken their minds, strengthen their muscles, lift their spirits, multiply their blessings, increase their opportunities, comfort their souls, raise up friends and pour out peace. Whoever will lose his life to God will find he has eternal life" ("Jesus Christ—Gifts and Expectations," Christmas Devotional, Salt Lake City, Utah, December 7, 1986). That's remarkable. Our Father will help us be able to do things we never thought we could do. He'll provide for us the very things we search for.

We probably have no idea how many reach out to us for help. Sometimes, if you're like me, you'll have a memory pop into your mind of a kindness someone has shown and you wonder where that person is now and what he or she is doing. And you wonder if the person knows how grateful you feel for the service given at a time when you needed it. President Spencer W. Kimball explained that when God answers our prayers he often sends another mortal to respond to our need. (See *The Teachings of Spencer W. Kimball* [Salt Lake City: Bookcraft, 1982], p. 252.)

Does Zonie know what it meant to me to have a best friend during my growing-up years? Her folks were Uncle Leo and Aunt Irene to me, and we spent fourteen years side by side, making popcorn and reading *Gone with the Wind* together, sleeping out under the stars and then telling ghost stories and getting so scared that we had to go into her house and sleep on the floor.

Does Mr. Halversen know the wonderful things he

awakened in my soul by patiently teaching me to play the violin and letting me participate in Handel's *Messiah* each year? He could have given up so many times. He weathered our marshmallow fights in the brand-new orchestra pit and trips on the bus to Beaver and Delta and other places to put on *La Traviata* and *Il Trovatore*. How did he do it?

Does Mr. Wynn know what a difference he made in my life in sixth grade by treating me as if I had some potential? In fifth grade I'd been branded as a child who had too many ideas and too little attention span. I got restless. I would finish my work and then get to the fun things: making little briefcases out of paper, inventing families with official documents for each member, like the records the ward clerk read at the pulpit when new families moved into the ward (I think I secretly always wanted to do that). My fifth-grade teacher told my parents that yes, my work was okay, but he just couldn't seem to keep me busy. Then how did Mr. Wynn do it? He had me write what I'd done last summer, prepare messages about safety to be read over the school PA system, work on extra spelling words, practice my printing, write about my family and friends. He encouraged me in some poems I wrote, and a few of them were published. He let me be on the boxing and tumbling teams when I didn't want to dance and braid the Maypole with the other girls. His style was encouragement and praise.

Many people have been instruments in God's hands along the way to help me find myself and stretch and grow. I'm grateful. I'm thankful God sometimes uses MEE as an instrument in His hands, too. They are safe hands. They know what they're doing. They know what I can do and what I can't. They know what this day, this season, is like for me. I like the way Alma expressed it in his "O that I were an angel" wish, recorded in Alma 29. In verse 9 he said: "I know that which the Lord hath commanded me, and I glory in it. I do not glory of myself, but I glory in that which the Lord hath commanded me; yea, and this is my glory, that perhaps I may be an instrument in the hands of God to bring some soul to repentance; and this is my joy." May it be our joy as well.

Chapter 5

THE MAGIC WAND

I HAD A GLORIOUSLY HAPPY childhood. I grew up (well, it didn't actually "take," and I changed my mind, deciding it was better not to grow up) in a wonderful small town that was just right for someone like me. There were lots of kids, lots of fields, lots of hills nearby, and lots of trees and bugs and stuff. Moms wore aprons, and houses had front porches. Winters brought lots of snow, and we could go all the way down our street on our sleds and sometimes "biz" cars (latch on to them and slide for a ways). In the summer we had lots of sunshine and water in the ditch for our boat races. They were just sticks, really, but we could imagine them into huge, beautiful pirate and trading ships. In our neighborhood the only ones I couldn't beat up on were the parents and the older boys. Life was good.

Then Sharon moved in up the street. She was a year older and a lot bigger than I was, and she started causing problems right away. One day she wouldn't let me use the swing when I was ready to. Another day she made fun of my braces. It was always something. She single-handedly disrupted my happy childhood.

I had to do something. So I decided to kill Sharon. I wasn't sure how to do that—we didn't have TV yet—but I did know that you don't want to leave evidence when you kill someone. If "they" find evidence, you could go to jail. I didn't want to go to jail. I liked Tony, our policeman, but I didn't want to spend all my time with him at the jail. I just wanted Sharon out of the way.

I began plotting how to kill Sharon without leaving evidence. I couldn't ask Charlotte or Paul; they'd tell. And I certainly couldn't ask my parents. They wouldn't understand. They wouldn't help. I had to do this one alone. But how?

Then one day I was reading a fairy tale in a big, beautifully illustrated book. On one page there was a fairy godmother who had a magic wand, and she waved it and POOF! Stars flew every direction, and magical things happened. And on the next page there were major changes— and no evidence. That was it! A magic wand! I would get a magic wand, kill Sharon (and who knows who else), and there would be no evidence.

But how was I going to get a magic wand? I began glancing around in the stores in town whenever I was there. No wands. I couldn't ask. Someone would surely remember that I had inquired about a magic wand shortly before Sharon's mysterious and untimely death. I had to do this on my own. It was the most major project I had ever undertaken, but I had to do it without help.

With my warped sense of faith I finally came to the conclusion that the way to get a magic wand was to pray for it. I was aware that it was a big request and felt I ought to do some special preparations in order to get ready to ask. So for a whole day I tried to be good and kind to everyone, including my mother and father and all my brothers and sisters. No small task. I could almost feel heaven smiling down on me and being thrilled that I was finally making some progress.

At last the moment seemed right for me to kneel down

by my bed. I didn't come right out and ask for a wand. First I kind of hinted about how good I'd been, pointing out some specific things I'd done that I felt were above and beyond what could reasonably be expected. Things that would have been normal procedure for others were second miles for me—big time.

And then I did it. I asked for a wand. I didn't tell Him what it was for. I finished my prayer and thought about the wand and Sharon as I drifted off to sleep that night. I came so close to telling Charlotte . . .

I gave Them a few days to make the wand before I started looking for it. I hadn't specified in my prayer where it should be delivered, so I didn't know where They'd drop it off. I began looking in all the wonderful places where I used to hide things throughout the neighborhood, but I couldn't find the wand. After a couple of days the thought struck me that maybe Charlotte had found the wand and was plotting something against me. So I looked in her stuff. Still couldn't find it.

Eventually I realized that I wasn't going to get the magic wand. I was so disappointed and frustrated. Sharon continued living in the neighborhood, and we eventually learned to get along. A few times I came close to telling her how lucky she was to still be alive.

Sometimes I still pray for magic wands. Not literally, of course, but I do desire some things that never get delivered in quite the way I had anticipated. Sometimes I'm so convinced of the absolute rightness of an idea that I forget one critical step: "Thy will be done." It's like my friend Dick has said: We sometimes present so many wonderful, ideal possibilities or recommendations to the Lord and then wait to see if he chooses A, or B, or even C or D. And the Lord chooses N or Q, and that makes all the difference, even when we don't immediately understand why.

One thing I didn't take into account in those years long ago was a verse from the Book of Mormon: "And whatsoever ye shall ask the Father in my name, which is right, believing that ye shall receive, behold it shall be given unto you" (3 Nephi 18:20). I hadn't yet learned the part about "which is right."

The same thing is taught in other verses, too. The Savior said: "Whatsoever thing ye shall ask the Father in my name, which is good, in faith believing that ye shall receive, behold, it shall be done unto you" (Moroni 7:26). King Benjamin reminds us: "And now, if God, who has created you, on whom you are dependent for your lives and for all that ye have and are, doth grant unto you whatsoever ye ask that is right, in faith, believing that ye shall receive, O then, how ye ought to impart of the substance that ye have one to another" (Mosiah 4:21).

It's not always easy to know what is right and good, to honestly say to Heavenly Father in our prayers, "Thy will be done." We get the feeling that a certain magic wand would be just what we need, and we pray earnestly, only to realize at some point that perhaps God knew all along that it wasn't best for us.

I went through an interesting exercise in understanding the Lord's will when I lost my scriptures on February 7, 1991. I wasn't too concerned right at first. When I realized at my office that they were missing, I knew they must be at home, or in the car, or in Salt Lake City at the Relief Society Building. I knew I would get them back. My name was in them. When I said to someone, "I lost my scriptures," they'd ask, "Well, where did you put them?" If I knew where I had put them they wouldn't be lost, but people still asked that question.

The last time I remembered having them was after a meeting at the Relief Society Building. My hands were full, and I stuck the scriptures, in their plastic holder-with-a-handle, on the top of the car. So I got thinking perhaps I had left them there. Agh! It was like the story of a family cruising down the freeway on their vacation. The wife looks over at the husband and asks, "Where's little Ralphie?" Oh no! He's on top of the car in his little holder, loving this vacation, his hair sticking straight out and drool going fifty-five miles an hour for miles behind him!

Anyway, it was a few days before I became concerned. Then I slowly realized that my scriptures weren't in any of the places where I thought they might be. Still I remained somewhat calm. Surely they would come back. Someone would find them and see my name and address and get in touch. Each time I drove to or from the Relief Society Building I looked carefully, going the same way I always went. I didn't want them to be in a ditch or alongside the road somewhere.

My next step was to imagine that, yes, someone had found my scriptures, and they were reading them, and they were in the process of conversion, and when they were ready to be baptized, they would get in touch, and it would be a fabulous story with an incredibly happy ending. Yes, that was what was happening. My scriptures were busy doing their thing.

But I missed them. I hadn't realized how much I liked them, that one particular set. I had gone through the trauma of switching to the new editions, giving up the Bible and the triple combination that my parents had given me long years before and that I had taken with me on my first mission. These new ones had been on a couple of missions with me. They had been to Asia and Africa. They smelled like mold, and it made me homesick and nostalgic whenever I caught their scent. I missed all the things I had written in the margins. I missed the way they seemed to pop open to just what I needed.

Of course I prayed for those scriptures. I'd had the magic-wand experience already, so I wasn't demanding or anything. I just let Heavenly Father know that I missed my scriptures and would sure love to get them back. And although I probably didn't exactly say, "Thy will be done," I did say, "If it's possible" or "If it's a good idea" or "If it would be okay." Of course, I couldn't imagine a single reason why it wouldn't be a wonderful idea for me to get them back.

Days passed and then weeks. I remembered a lot of things about scriptures in my life. Like when I was little and people used to get up in church meetings and say how much they loved the scriptures and I used to think things like, "That's a big, fat lie." I would try to read them. I don't think we were encouraged then as much as we are now to study our scriptures. People used to joke that if all the Mormons took their copies of the Book of Mormon off their shelves at the same time and blew off the dust, there would be an eclipse.

Sometimes I would start reading and get Lehi and his family out in the desert and then get bored with all they were doing. I got impatient with their having to send the boys back for plates and people. Why didn't they think of those things in the first place? Didn't Jerusalem sell day planners?

When I got a little older, I got some encouragement from seminary. I set a goal to have my black, paperback copy of the Book of Mormon all red. (That's *red*, not *read*.) My desire was to have other people look over when I opened the book and be impressed out of their minds because I had colored the whole thing red. I didn't particularly care at the time what was in it, but I sure wanted to impress others. I used my ruler and a whole bunch of red marking pens, and wow! It was impressive, all right. I kept it as a reminder, and when I look at it now I realize that the only parts that stand out are the parts I left white. Ha.

Well, general conference was getting closer, and I still had not found my scriptures. Eventually it was as if the still small voice said something to me like, "Edmunds, get a grip. They're gone. You've got to get some more." And so I did. Shortly before conference I bought a whole set. I tried to like them—not very hard, but I did try. They weren't user friendly. They wouldn't pop open to the right place. They didn't smell like mold. Nothing was written in the margins. And for some reason I didn't write my name in them. Not yet. I did take them to conference and other places with me. I tried to bond with them. It wasn't working.

A few days after conference, when my *real* scriptures had been gone two months, I had a feeling that I wanted to pray about them again. I hadn't mentioned them in several weeks because I didn't want to be too pushy. But on an evening in April when I knelt to pray I included something about my scriptures. I said to Heavenly Father, "I know You can see them." I knew He knew where they were. I didn't say it like, "So why haven't You brought them back?" It was just something I knew. And I asked for the last time about getting them back. He knew it was the last time. I mentioned how much I had missed them and how I hadn't realized how much that particular set meant to me. I thanked Him for not being mad at me for bringing it up again and told Him I would let go if for some reason they couldn't come back. I wouldn't bother Him again about that particular subject.

The next morning I got to the Missionary Training Center early. Since the door near my office was locked, I walked through the lobby. I decided to check my mailbox while I was so near the front desk. In it was a green slip, one of those forms that says "An item for you that would not fit in your mailbox has been placed above the mailboxes. The item is . . . " The blank was filled in with red pen: "your scriptures." What?

I looked up, and sure enough, there they were. No plastic cover, but I recognized them instantly. I grabbed them and ran down the hall to my office. I hardly had time to shut and lock the door before I started crying—hard. I knelt and thanked Heavenly Father for answering my prayers. Imagine how Heavenly Father can look down on all His billions of children and pick us out, one by one, knowing our names and our needs, and responding in such unusual (sometimes we say "mysterious" when we don't comprehend the particulars), specific, remarkable, miraculous ways. I keep the green slip inside my scriptures (it now smells a little like mold too) and it reminds me of many things but mostly of how loving and patient and merciful God is with us and how well He knows each of us.

Heavenly Father didn't give me a magic wand, but He has been unfailingly generous in giving me many other things. He always answers me, even though sometimes He says no, or later, or we'll see. I have come to the realization that too many times in my life when He has said no, as with the magic wand, I've been convinced that my prayers weren't answered. Not so. There are things I have prayed for with all my heart, as hard and earnestly as I knew how, and then I've had to trust that the prayer will be answered but maybe not with the answer I hoped for.

Incidentally, my dear friend Subandriyo (we call him Yoyo) from Indonesia happened to be at general conference that year. When I saw him after I had found my scriptures, I asked if he had a set in English. He said no, but he surely would like one someday. Not all the books have been translated into Indonesian, and he enjoys things like the Topical

Guide. I told him about my experience and gave him my newly purchased scriptures, saying how nice it was that I would just happen to have an extra set. He smiled as only he can and said, "Oh, Sister, the Lord works in mysterious ways. He knew that Yoyo needed some English scriptures." Yes, He did.

Elder H. Burke Peterson has said, "I wonder sometimes if we are willing to pay the price for an answer from the Lord" (*Ensign*, January 1974, p. 19). He made me wonder what the price might be for an answer from the Lord. Listening? Obeying? Working hard to know what is right and good? Thanking Him more often and more genuinely? Elder Peterson also said that "prayer is the preparation for miracles." And indeed it is. I have experienced many miracles in my life—precious, small things and a few rather big things. Yet some things that I thought would happen haven't.

I worked through some concerns about all of this when I was serving as a missionary. I thought that if I worked hard enough, prayed with enough faith, and did the best I could, Big Miracles would happen. I think I wanted to be able to write a journal entry something like this:

"One day we got up, and we were prompted to eat rice for breakfast, and then we felt we should go tracting, and then we saw some clouds in the sky that formed a house number, and we went there, and a family was sitting in their living room dressed all in white, waiting for us, and they had their tithing in a powdered milk can, and they'd had a dream, and we were in the dream, and they recognized us immediately, and we started telling them about Joseph Smith, and the wife burst into tears because her great-great-great-grandmother had found a Joseph Smith tract in the Old Country as she was digging up her yams, and it was in her tribal language, which, incidentally, is not one of the ninety-eight languages in which the tract is currently printed . . . "

Well, that didn't happen to me. But before I became a missionary I thought it likely would. I had listened to many missionaries give their homecoming messages, and when two years' experiences are condensed into twenty minutes, you hear of some wonderful miracles. I found that mission-ary work is *work*—hard work, hour by hour, day by day—and that even though I prayed for people with all my heart, things didn't always work out the way I hoped. And yet I have seen many miracles, and I am awfully glad I kept jour-nals on my missions, because you don't always know when you're at the beginning of, or in the middle of, or are some other part of a miracle. There's not always a loud announce-ment from heaven: "Here it comes! This is it!" Miracles are usually quiet, wonderful, and easily missed.

At the BYU Women's Conference on March 12, 1987, Sister Pat Holland shared some profound thoughts about prayer: "[Prayer] ought not to seem just a convenient and contrived miracle, for if we are to search for real light and eternal certainties, we have to pray as the ancients prayed. We are women now, not children, and are expected to pray with maturity. The words most often used to describe urgent, prayerful labor are *wrestle*, *plead*, *cry*, and *hunger*. In some sense, prayer may be the hardest work we will ever be engaged in, and perhaps it should be. It is pivotal protection against becoming so involved with worldly possessions and honors and status that we no longer desire to undertake the search for our soul" (*On Earth as It Is in Heaven* [Salt Lake City: Deseret Book, 1989], pp. 88–89).

Why don't we just talk and share more with our Heavenly Father? Do you think maybe sometimes we don't really believe that God does hear and understand us and that He will actually answer us? Are we nervous about talking to Him? I'm convinced that our Heavenly Father doesn't sit somewhere up there watching for us to make mistakes, watching for our imperfections—He's not trying to catch us doing something wrong. He wants to catch us doing things that are right and good, and then He says, "Way to go! You're all right!"

Too many of us seem to think of God as being disappointed or disgusted with us. We prayed for a magic wand. He said no. There can be no hope from now on. No, I don't think that's how it is. He allows us to learn and progress. He is pleased with our progress, our increase in awareness, our desire to truly communicate with Him.

It's unfair to imagine that God has anything but unconditional love for us, His children. He wants us to succeed. He does listen, understand, and respond to all the yearnings of our souls and each prayer we offer. There is nothing you or I could do that would cause God to stop loving us. Nothing. His love is unconditional, and we work to have that same kind of love for others.

It strikes me as pure genius that Heavenly Father asks us to pray for our enemies. Think of someone you've been mad at or feel far away from, and not just geographically. Include that individual in your prayers. Say his or her name. Pray to understand the person, to love him or her more, to think of just the right thing to do or say. What happens to you inside?

A headline in a news article from the Provo *Daily Herald* of January 13, 1994, caught my eye: "Try praying this year." Amazing. The article started out: "Looking for a happier New Year? A recent university study examining what contributes to a greater sense of well-being found a curious factor: certain types of prayer." Well, what do you know. A sociologist had surveyed over five hundred adults and had come up with the idea that prayer makes a difference.

"Frequent prayer heightens happiness, general life satisfaction, and religious satisfaction." True. With or without a survey, it's true.

We have a living, real Heavenly Father who wants to hear from us—often. It would be wonderful if we could talk to Him now the way we'll talk to Him when we see Him again—if we could just be real and genuine, open and trusting. Listening. Thanking. Asking. Waiting. Knowing He'll never ask us to do anything stupid, anything we can't do, anything that doesn't matter. He asks that we ask, seek, and knock, and He promises to respond. And God has never broken a promise.

Chapter 6

BEATRICE

I WENT TO SIXTH GRADE IN the new East Elementary. We had to cross Main Street to get there, but other than that it was a great place. Many of my best friends had transferred there with me the year before when the school was first opened. I liked all the space around the school—there was plenty of room for games of war during recess.

One day when I came home from school my mother asked me an interesting question: "Is Beatrice in your class?" I answered yes in a tone like "Who wants to know?" She said, "Tell me about Beatrice," so I told her that Beatrice had a crooked back and heart trouble. Mom asked me to tell her more and then asked questions seemingly aimed at finding out whether or not I was a friend to Beatrice—if I was aware of her and kind to her.

Mom asked what I did at recess, and I answered with enthusiasm, "We play war!" She asked what Beatrice did at recess. "She watches us play war." "Doesn't she play with you?" "No, she just watches us. She has a crooked back and heart trouble so she can't play war." Mom said, "Does anyone spend time with her, or is she alone?" I explained (trying to be patient) that we were all busy playing war, and Beatrice just sat and watched us.

Mom said something like, "Well, that must get very

lonely, just watching everyone else play. Don't you ever spend time with her?" I couldn't believe she didn't already know or guess the answer to that one. "Mom! I'm a general!" We took safety pins and wrapped different colors of yarn around them to indicate our rank. I had three or four of those safety pins, indicating that I was a general.

Mom didn't comprehend the significance of my being a general. "Well," she persisted, "I just think it would be kind if you spent some time with Beatrice. I don't think it's right that she should spend all her time alone at recess. I think she must get lonely sometimes." I guess Mom thought it was no great thing to be a general—that it didn't take much effort. I tried to explain to her that if I didn't play hard every recess there was no way I could continue being a general. It was a Big Deal.

But her words stayed with me. I began to notice Beatrice watching us at recess, mostly sitting alone quietly. Once I even went and sat down beside her and talked for a few minutes. She was nice. But then I had to get back to the war; generals might be needed at any moment.

Some time went by, and then one day Mom asked, "Was Beatrice in class today?" I said that she wasn't and that she hadn't been at school for several days. Mom asked, "Do you know where she is?" I didn't know that Mom knew where she was and just wanted to find out if I knew. I answered something like, "Maybe she died." Mom said, "No, no, she hasn't died. But she's very sick, and she's home, and they're going to have to take her to the Primary Children's Hospital to have surgery." I didn't know that.

Then Mom said she was going to go visit Beatrice and wondered if I wanted to go along. I responded, "But Mom— she lives in Dog Town!" We probably called that part of the city Dog Town for several reasons: Some of the roads weren't paved yet, and not all the families had indoor plumbing. I was wondering what would happen if any of my soldiers saw their general in Dog Town. Mom finally said, "I'll just go alone then."

Well, I couldn't let my mother go to Dog Town alone. I thought about it for a while and then said, "Mom, I'll go with you." She said, "Why don't you take some of your toys to Beatrice. They have a lot of children and not much money, and I'm sure she'd appreciate getting something from you that she could play with and maybe take to the hospital with her." Oh my. Giving up toys. This was a big request.

Then I remembered that my younger sister Charlotte wasn't home. I gathered a few of her toys in a sack and called downstairs to let Mom know I was ready. She wasn't finished with me, though. "Mary Ellen, why don't you take Beatrice one of your favorite toys. If it's one of your favorite toys I'm sure she'd enjoy it too." Oh, yikes. Now what would I do?

I couldn't imagine taking Beatrice my very favorite toy, my Grasshopper Hospital. Oh, what a fun, fun toy! Mom didn't want it at our place, and we didn't have a very good front porch for it anyway. But Uncle Leo and Aunt Irene had the perfect porch for my hospital, so I had set it up there.

I would capture grasshoppers and throw them on the ground, usually on cement. Splunk! Of course they'd be injured and need hospitalization. I had made some little beds from cardboard, and I would put each grasshopper on a bed. I used toilet paper for blankies and covered them up. Then, because I had learned lots of words from my dad, a doctor, I knew exactly what to write on the chart by each 'hopper: "Critical," "Coma," "Stroke," "Serious," and so on. And I watched over the grasshoppers.

Sometimes they would start to get better and act like they

didn't want to remain in bed! So down they'd go again: "Kaplunk!" And back to bed. Some of them quit participating. They died. So I had to open up a little cemetery in Grandma Chamberlain's backyard. I buried a lot of grasshoppers and other critters in that cemetery as the years went by.

Anyway, I knew I couldn't transport this favorite toy, my Grasshopper Hospital, over to Beatrice's house. And who knows if her mother would have let her keep it anyway. I didn't want to put those 'hoppers in any kind of danger, after all.

My next-favorite toy at the time may not seem significant to those who didn't grow up BTV (Before Television). It was a numbers game, the kind where you have numbers from one to fifteen in a little plastic case, and the object of the game is to shift the numbers around so you get them in order either horizontally or vertically. I loved setting world records, although no one ever knew about the records I set.

It was not with a burning sense of charity that I put my numbers game in the sack with Charlotte's toys. But at the same time, I know it didn't occur to me that I could get another numbers game if I gave this one to Beatrice. I was really giving it away; this was a true sacrifice if not exactly a charitable one.

I was ready now, so I went down and got in the car with Mom, and we drove over to Dog Town. I hadn't ever been to Beatrice's house before, and it caught me off guard when we pulled up in front. "This is where she lives?" "Yes." "Mom, it's so small!" "I know." "How many live here?" "They have nine children, I think." "Eleven people live in this small place?" "Yes." "Mom, that would be worse than sharing a room with Charlotte!" "Almost."

We went in, and it seemed like there were beds everywhere. There were no more than three rooms. I was looking around in amazement, probably with my mouth wide open and a stupid look on my face. This was a brand-new experience for me. I saw Beatrice in one of the beds, looking quite small and rather pale.

Finally my mother rescued me from my shock. "Beatrice, Mary Ellen brought you some toys." "Oh, yes!" I recovered somewhat and went over to the bed and handed her the sack. She looked inside and saw the numbers game right there on top. She was excited. "Oh, I've always wanted one of these," she said, and she pulled it out and began to experiment with it.

Something happened inside of me at that moment—something significant. I was too tough to let it show on the outside, but in my heart something very important and good was happening. I felt happy. I felt I'd done something that mattered. I felt close to Beatrice and close to my mom. The general was having a softening-of-the-heart experience.

I don't remember much else about the visit to Beatrice. I don't remember the ride home or anything that my mother might have said to me or that I might have said to her. I do remember that Beatrice went to the Primary Children's Hospital. Her picture was on the cover of the *Church News* as one of the first patients in the new facility.

My mother had me write to Beatrice. I didn't know what to say. "Hi. How's the food? Are they nice to you? Is it fun to have so many operations?" I'd write things like that, and she would answer. Sometimes when she had a break from the hospital her mother would bring her to visit us. She never came back to our school, though, and gradually we lost track of each other.

Many years later, KSL Radio advertised a contest they were running as some kind of promotion for a bank. It was called Citizen of the Week. You nominated someone as the Citizen of the Week, and if that person won, you and your nominee each received fifty dollars in a savings account at the bank.

"Hey, this is great," I thought. "I'll nominate my mother!" So I wrote up some things about her, like how she was a Silver Beaver and a nurse and all. I thought of a lot of excellent things to include. And she won! For a whole week on KSL Radio they said things like, "Ella M. Edmunds of Mapleton, Utah, is our Citizen of the Week. She was nominated by her lovely and talented . . . " Okay, they didn't really say those things about me, but they did mention my name.

It just so happened that our friend Beatrice was living in Salt Lake at the time, and she heard the announcement on the radio. She sent a letter to my mother and me, thanking us for the kindness we had shown to her those many years ago when she was a sometimes lonely sixth grader at East Elementary. I remember sitting in the living room with Mom, reading the letter and remembering. And it was one time when I honestly had to say, "My mother made me do it."

Beatrice and I have kept in touch since. I feel such gratitude for what she helped me learn when I was a general and CEO of the Grasshopper Hospital and hadn't yet had much of a taste of compassion. She seems to have forgiven me for all the times when I ignored her, when I was more concerned about being a general than being a Christian.

A few years ago I felt that I wanted to thank Beatrice specifically for the help she had given me. I had her address but not a phone number. So I wrote and asked her for her phone number. She sent it, and I called her. I said, "I want to come and go to church with you on Sunday." She seemed surprised. I explained that I had something I wanted to tell her.

She picked me up at the place where I was staying, and

we drove to the chapel together. It's not possible to adequately explain my feelings as I sat visiting with her and having so many memories come flooding back. She still had a somewhat crooked back and said she still had some problems with her heart. In fact, just a couple of years before that she had had some valves replaced with mechanical devices. I could hear them clicking during the silent times at church as I sat next to her.

I loved watching her interact with her friends. Many years had gone by since I'd been with her, so we had a lot of catching up to do. She had married and had two sons. Her husband had passed away from a brain tumor. She had lived in the same small home for more than twenty-five years. Most of those years she had served as the meetinghouse librarian in her ward. Everyone knew her. I enjoyed watching and listening as she responded to questions and greeted different ward members.

We sat together in sacrament meeting, Sunday School, and Relief Society. My feelings were very tender and deep. I knew what I wanted to tell her, but I didn't know quite how to make it come out right.

When the meetings finished, we went back to her car. She drove me back to where I was staying, and then we began to share. I felt weepy. This was an important experience for me. I told her I wanted to bring back a memory from sixth grade and see if she remembered anything about it. I told her the whole story, including every detail I could think of. I told her about what my mom had said, and how I had started noticing her more but hadn't been as good a friend as I had since wished I had been. I told her about visiting in her home with my mom and about the numbers game.

I thanked her as honestly as I knew how for the effect she'd had in my life at a time when I so much needed to feel what I felt. I asked if she remembered that. She said she didn't, although she did remember that we had written to each other while she was in the Primary Children's Hospital. She asked, "Do you want me to tell you the first thing I remember about you?" I didn't know if I wanted her to or not; I had been such a wild, tough kid. But I decided to risk. "Yes. What do you remember about me?"

She said it was on one of our field days at school. Those were such fun days—girls got to wear pants! And we got to play outside the whole day. Beatrice remembered that we were sitting around a fire roasting marshmallows. She said, "I didn't have any. We were too poor even to buy marshmallows. And you shared yours with me."

Well, the tears came. I felt so thankful that her first memory of me wasn't something like, "You were a general, and I watched you play, day after day, wishing I could come and join you." I had shared my marshmallows. Oh, thank goodness.

Thank you, Beatrice, for the ways in which you have blessed and enriched me. Your friendship means a lot to me. You made a difference in my life. I'm glad for times when mothers and fathers and others seem to know just what we need. I'm grateful that they encourage us to do what is right and good. I'm thankful for friends and neighbors who somehow are able to be patient with us while we learn, often very slowly, how to be kinder and more aware.

Chapter 7

THE WAIT-A-WHILE CLUB

A LONG TIME AGO, I figured out that my sister Charlotte generally got a lot more out of meetings than I did. She noticed things—and people—I missed. She was paying attention. I wanted to be more like her in that regard.

A related observation was that people seemed really to thrive on compliments, even (or perhaps especially) if those compliments came sometime after the fact, rather than simply on the spur of the moment. I've talked to lots of people who have treasured notes of encouragement and thanks they have received. I have several such notes myself. They arrived after a while, when someone remembered something specific about a talk or an experience and took the time to mention it.

From those two observations was born the idea of the Wait-a-While Club. It's a great club, because there are no meetings or dues. There are, however, some responsibilities. People who join the Wait-a-While Club have got to pay attention as the days go by. Members are always on the lookout for ways to lift someone—to say thanks, to give encouragement, to express love.

Several years ago I was in northern California speaking at a fireside during which I had decided to invite people to join the Wait-a-While Club. I had picked out someone sitting right on the front row to help me in a little role-playing situation. When I went to pick on her, though, some invisible hand had pushed her head down. Ooops! So I gazed down the bench a little farther and was strongly prompted to ask another woman sitting there if I could pick on her. I had noticed her before the meeting began—I was sitting in the foyer when she came in, and for some reason I watched her and wondered who she was.

I asked if I could use her for a kind of example. She nodded. I asked her what her first name was, and she answered, "Betty." I asked, "Betty, do you get nervous when you give a talk or teach a lesson or something like that?"

She hesitated momentarily and then responded, "I'm not sure—I've never done anything like that." Wow, I thought. How has she lived this long without ever giving a talk or teaching a lesson? I've gotta talk to her!

But I went on. "Let's suppose you would be nervous," I suggested, and she said it would be easy to suppose that.

My next question is usually something like, "How could I tell you were nervous?" People often give such answers as "My mouth gets dry," "My neck goes red," "I fiddle with my necklace," "My voice sounds shaky," or whatever. I mentioned that some of those things might happen to Betty, and we could then tell that she was nervous.

I said, "Let's suppose, Betty, that you have given a talk about faith. We'll pretend that I said something nice after the meeting, but we'll also pretend that I come up to you after a while. Maybe it's been a week. I ask if you have a moment to talk, and you say yes. Then I offer a specific compliment about your talk, something like this: 'Betty, thank you for your talk on faith last week. It meant a lot to me. I especially appreciated the experience you shared about you and your father and what you learned about faith. I hope you don't mind, but I wrote that in my journal.'"

I asked Betty what that might mean to her. She responded very positively, saying it would mean everything to know that someone had remembered and was helped by something specific she had said.

Then I invited everyone at the fireside to join the club. I encouraged them all to watch for opportunities to give praise and positive comments and thanks to others, particularly those who might have a special need for a lift.

After the meeting Betty waited until most of the people had left, and then she came up to say something. I hugged her (it being National Hug Day—as it is every day for me) and she whispered, "I've been out of the Church for fifty years." "Fifty years!" "Yes." "Oh, Betty, welcome back! Welcome home!" I hugged her hard.

She said with emotion, "Think of all I've missed! I have so much to learn and so much to do." I said, "That's true for all of us, Betty." I kept hugging her and saying, "Welcome back, Betty. Welcome home." I couldn't believe it; I was overcome by my feelings. She'd been away for almost as long as I had been alive. And now she had come back. She asked if I would pray for her, and I promised I would.

After I returned home I kept thinking about Betty. I had a strong desire to keep in touch with her, to let her know that I was praying for her, and to find out how she was. But I didn't even know her last name. I contacted the stake Relief Society president in California, and she helped me get Betty's address. I wrote her a letter, sharing some of my feelings and asking how she was.

I heard from Betty in August 1991. I laughed when she said she saw the Missionary Training Center envelope and thought she had been called on a mission! She wrote in her letter: "How can that be? I've only been back in the Church two months!" She told me a lot about her life, and it sure hadn't been an easy one.

She said, "I'm happy I have been on your mind. Your willingness to pray for me has put me there. As I begin my walk down that 'narrow way,' *now* is when I feel I most need the strength of others' prayers. So, please remember me. . . . I'm the one who was wandering in the wilderness, in absolute misery, for so many, many years."

She told me how it happened that she came back. "Every Easter I watch the TV religious programs. This past Easter was different. While watching, I felt uncomfortable, restless, and terribly sad. I cried during the Crucifixion. I had never cried before, and I'd been watching these programs for decades.

"May 31, 1991, was a Friday like any other (I thought). No one could have been more surprised than I to come home from work, walk right to the telephone directory, and call the first ward number I saw."

She said that several weeks later her cousin Dorothy mailed some baptismal information she had kept through all the years. "It was then that I saw my baptismal date of May 31, 1941!" Imagine! It's as if Someone decided that after exactly fifty years it was time to help Betty come back.

"I am currently studying my beginner and transitional lessons," Betty wrote. "My visiting teachers come every Wednesday evening." One thing that struck me was that those visiting teachers were focused on Betty, not on what "counted" or what they might get credit for. Betty mattered more than the fact that they were visiting her more often than might have been recommended in some guidelines somewhere. She needed them; so, they came.

"I have read the Book of Mormon," she continued, "and I am really learning. I am aware of that 'other' Betty disappearing and the 'new' Betty emerging." She asked me to please continue to keep her in my thoughts and prayers and "remember me especially when you hear my favorite hymn, 'I Stand All Amazed.'"

I've kept in touch with Betty. She lives in Utah now, and we've had the privilege of going to the temple together. She attends the temple each week and is working in family history. She has shared her testimony and experiences in many settings. She expresses great joy at each new thing she discovers. She read *Jesus the Christ* and was absolutely thrilled at what she learned about the Savior. A friend of hers, her visiting teaching companion, lends her books.

I'm grateful to Betty for helping me to have so much joy and so many interesting adventures because of my membership in the Wait-a-While Club.

In 1992 during BYU Education Week I met Robert and Alan, two buddies almost seventeen years old who came to all my classes. That surprised me. I couldn't imagine that anyone would be that interested, especially someone aged sixteen. We became friends right away. Something about them impressed me very much. I knew, for example, that they were Wait-a-While Club members. They had joined much earlier in their lives than I had. One day they gave a note to the hostess who was helping in the room. They thanked her for her efforts, telling her they noticed that everyone thanked the speaker but forgot about the help she had given. Unusual. Who were these young men?

We've kept in touch. Once they both borrowed suits and I showed them around the Missionary Training Center. They came back to Education Week in 1993 as hosts and brought some of their friends. They invited me to be present when they were ordained elders, which I was thrilled to do. Alan became an elder first, and then a few days later he helped ordain Robert. Robert is serving a mission in

California now, and Alan's in Brazil. Before leaving they were team teachers for a class in family history work in their singles ward. They helped one sister submit five hundred names to the temple. I'm keeping my eyes on these club members; they're extraordinary!

I've met many lifers—people who have been in the club for their whole lives and didn't even know it. One of these is Nancy, whom I met in January 1992 when she was in the MTC preparing to go on a mission. We were talking about the club, and she said, "I think I'm a member." One of the things she does whenever she visits a ward is to look for the one who is playing the prelude music and give that person a positive comment before leaving the chapel. One time she realized that the woman who was playing the prelude music was just kind of propped up on the bench. After Nancy mentioned how much she appreciated the prelude music, the woman sat up and put her whole heart into the playing!

Nancy also told of a young man in her ward who one week had to try four times before he got the sacrament prayer right. He was extremely embarrassed. She went up to him when she got a chance and thanked him for blessing the sacrament four times. She said to him, "I wasn't ready the first three times . . . thank you for doing it four times so that I could prepare myself to partake of the sacrament with the right spirit." She told him he had helped her to have one of the most significant experiences she'd ever had in participating in that sacred ordinance. That made a big difference for him and for her. Hooray for all the members of the Wait-a-While Club!

Have you ever saved a note you've received? Maybe it was a note thanking you for something you did, or for your influence, or for some specific experience or event. Perhaps you have a memory of a phone call or a visit with someone who thanked you or remembered you in a specific way.

Can you think of people you have meant to thank? Have you waited quite a while? Are there letters you've meant to write, visits you've meant to make, phone calls on a list somewhere? Even if it's been a long, long while, it's never too late to thank someone.

Think of the people who have had a significant influence in your life. Here's a little exercise to try: sit down and give it some careful thought and then make a list of everyone you can think of who has made a difference in your life. Of course, each time we do that, we'll probably leave out someone who deserves to be on our list. Hundreds of people influence us. But it's a sweet feeling when we start to name names and remember.

Besides your family and your Heavenly Father and the Savior and the Holy Ghost, who has had the greatest influence on your life? As you write down each name, consider why you included that person on your list. Has it been a while since you made an effort to thank the people you've thought of?

Are there people in your life who have helped you whom you have never thanked? It's not like they're waiting—keeping a list and checking it off when the thank-you's pour in. But I wonder what it would mean to them to receive a note, a phone call, even a visit where that's possible. You won't be able to get in touch with some of them, certainly. Maybe they've gone Home (died). Maybe they've moved, and you've just lost track of them. Write a thank-you note anyway, even if you can't send it. It just might turn out to be one of the sweetest experiences you've had in a long time. And then try another thing: Write a letter from *them* to *you*. What would they say? What would they remember about you? What would they want you to know? What counsel might they give you?

Years ago I wrote my mother a letter as if it came from *her* mother, who died in 1942 when my mother was just twenty-seven years old. Mother had mentioned to me many times how much she missed her mother. I don't know where the idea came from, but I wrote her a letter as if it were from her mother, telling her how well she had done as a wife and mother as well as a daughter.

Another time I wrote a long letter to my brother Richard's first child, "little Richard," telling him all about his father. It probably meant more to me than it did to that little newborn baby (or his parents) to have had the sweet experience of writing that letter.

My list of those to whom I owe much includes my parents, of course, and I've never been able to thank them adequately for their remarkable wisdom, their patience and love, their endless second and third miles. Each brother and sister has influenced me in specific, wonderful ways. Friends, teachers, companions—people I've known almost my whole life and people who came and went in a few minutes—all have left unforgettable impressions and powerful lessons.

People I've never met have influenced me in significant ways, like Gandhi, Mother Teresa, Helen Keller and her teacher Anne Sullivan, Albert Schweitzer, and others who are quite famous. Many people know their names and feel their influence. But my list also contains many names that wouldn't be so easily recognized.

Will someone name your name some day? "She was my Primary teacher." "He was my next-door neighbor." "This is the family that welcomed me and made me feel so comfortable and safe." "She was my high school English teacher." "He wasn't just my brother; he was my friend." "It all started the day I had a flat tire on my way to school." "It might have seemed to her like a little thing, but it has made all the difference for me."

If you've been a member of the Wait-a-While Club for a

while, carry on. If you're just joining, welcome. You're going to love this. And if you're still thinking about becoming a member, realizing it does take some effort, you can't imagine how much fun this is. Join us! All it takes is caring and doing, feeling and then acting upon those feelings, watching for the chance to give someone genuine praise and encouragement. The blessings will come back to you; they always, always do.

Chapter 8

AUNT FLORENCE

WE LEARN FROM WATCHING OTHERS, and often they don't even know they're providing a learning experience for us. Some of the most wonderful examples of love I have seen have come from people who didn't know I was watching.

One day when I was coming out of the BYU Creamery I witnessed a scene I'll remember forever. I saw a father and mother with their children. The father was holding one small child in his arms and had the hand of another, a little girl about three years old. The mother was headed back toward the car with a child a little older, maybe four or five, who was not a happy camper. She had apparently misbehaved and was evidently not going to be allowed to participate in the creamery experience with the rest of them.

The little one holding her dad's hand was visibly upset. "Don't! Don't make her go back!" she cried, looking up at her father and then back at her mother and sister. "She won't do it again! She's sorry!" So far she wasn't getting any results (except she had me almost in tears and the father and mother seemed to be reconsidering). Then came the clincher: "*Please!* She's sorry! She won't do it again! I pwomise! I pwomise!" That did it. The mother brought the

76

sister back, and the whole team went into the creamery. I was deeply touched. Saved by a Sunbeam!

One of the most powerful seminars on love I ever attended was the funeral service for Sharmayn Ferguson several years ago. Sharmayn had cystic fibrosis and died at age eleven. She had put an amazing amount of living into those eleven years, with the extraordinary help and encouragement of her parents, Ike and Gloria, and the rest of her family, neighbors, and friends. I learned a great deal about love from Sharmayn's life. I had seen her many times. Often she went with her dad to ward dinners and other functions. She loved life. She packed the hours and days as full as she could. She roller-skated with an IV in her arm and played softball hooked up to a portable oxygen unit. She was unusually sensitive to others of all ages and kind and compassionate in wonderful ways. She had a hope of someday discovering a cure for something.

I sensed in the years I knew Sharmayn that she knew she wouldn't live long but had chosen not to sit around and be upset about it. She wanted to experience as much as she could, and she almost ignored her physical challenges. I loved watching the relationship between Sharmayn and her parents, her older brother, Shawn, and her little sister, Kiera. She was there when Shawn got his Eagle Scout award. That was one of her important goals. A tender account of her life, entitled "Sharmayn's Farewell," was written by her dad, Isaac Ferguson, and published in the January 1982 *Ensign*, page 54. Reading it will enrich you and bless you and help you understand more about love as a verb.

The same is true of an article written by my dear friend and missionary companion, Mary Jane Hawkes, about her precious little Sarah, who was able to stay with her family for only a few years. Her story is told in "Sharing Sarah: Our Down's Syndrome Baby," *Ensign*, June 1981, page 32. I met sweet Sarah just a couple of times, but she had a way of making it right to your heart and leaving a lasting impression of love, of a bright spirit, and of a wonderful future awaiting.

When I think about loving life, I often think of my Aunt Florence. What a happy, wonderful soul. She wasn't really my aunt but my father's second cousin, Florence Sperry. She was born in Manti, Sanpete County, Utah, on September 1, 1892. My first memories of her were in small number 29 at the Kimball Apartments on north Main Street in Salt Lake City.

Occasionally we traveled all the way from Mapleton to that big city to visit. For a while Aunt Florence cared for her father, Harry Sperry, who occupied a bed near the window. She also cared for her mother, but I have no memory of that. Florence lived alone in number 29 for about thirty-five years. She was quite a fixture in the neighborhood, and everyone in the Kimball and the Jensen apartments knew her. She was an election judge for many years and could call most of her neighbors by name (and tell more about them than they probably would have wished).

Aunt Florence was a schoolteacher. She taught music in places like the Jordan School District, Ogden, and Price. She played the violin and sang baritone—yes, baritone!— with her deep, rich voice. I loved seeing her pictures from when she sang in a male chorus and when she played the leading man in an opera.

In 1965, several months after returning from a mission, I began teaching at the Missionary Home in Salt Lake City. It was located in the old Ute Hotel, right across the street from the Kimball Apartments where Aunt Florence lived. Twice a week I went to teach at the Missionary Home and visited with Aunt Florence in number 29. Sometimes she needed me to run some errands, such as shopping for a few groceries at the store on the northwest corner of North Temple and Main.

On Tuesday evenings I went to Aunt Florence's before I taught, because it was late by the time I finished, and I was teaching nursing at BYU at the time and had to be at the hospital with students by 6:15 A.M. on Wednesdays. So I visited Aunt Florence before teaching and then headed straight home when I finished at the Missionary Home. One Tuesday when I finished teaching at about 9:15 P.M., I had a strong impression that I should go back across the street to Aunt Florence's. I resisted it at first because I'd already had a good visit with her, I was tired, and it was a long drive back to Provo.

The impression became stronger, and finally I obeyed. When I knocked on her door she called out, "Oh, Mary Ellen! Is that you?" She had fallen and couldn't get up. She'd been praying that I would come back, even though I usually didn't. She needed me to go to the office, get a key to her apartment, and come back and help her. I did so immediately and stayed with her a little while. We both cried about that answer to her prayer.

Aunt Florence and I grew very close during the years I taught at the Missionary Home and visited her each week. We had such fun during our visits. Sometimes when I knocked she made extra sure it was me before she would open the door because, she would protest, "I don't have my eyebrows on yet!" She was a large woman who looked terrific when she dressed up.

Often I found Aunt Florence sitting near the window, writing something in one of her many notebooks. She kept track of the weather each day, among many other things. And she had some soap operas that she followed for years. She couldn't stand to miss them. When she stayed with us in Mapleton she had to plan everything around those programs. That was before VCRs, and she couldn't skip one episode for fear she would miss something critical or get behind on the story. She talked about the people in the soaps as if she knew them personally.

Another thing Aunt Florence kept track of was the Utah Stars, then our state's professional basketball team. They were born in Salt Lake City in about 1970, and she became an instant fan. She listened to every single game on her radio and soon was crazy (her word) about Bill Howard, the announcer, and "Z," Zelmo Beatty, one of the players. Even hospitalization didn't break her regular "attendance" at the Stars' games; in 1971 when she had surgery on her eye, she tuned in. One nurse remarked that Florence knew more about the team than the coach did.

Aunt Florence had a personal interest in each of the Stars' players. She talked about them as if they were her sons. She was genuinely upset when one of her favorites was traded or got injured or had an off night. In one of her small notebooks she carefully recorded the score each quarter during every game. She cut out and saved every newspaper article about the Stars. During their games she took her phone off the hook and shut out everyone and everything except the Stars and Bill Howard. She had a Stars bumper sticker plastered on the inside of her apartment door.

We suggested a few times that Aunt Florence should really go to a game in person, but by then she'd had a slight stroke and felt it was out of the question to "stumble over to the Salt Palace." Yet I could tell whenever we talked about it that she wished she could go.

Then along came Mark, a high-school senior looking for a service project for himself and some buddies in his priests quorum. It had been suggested to them that they might take Aunt Florence to see the Stars—and somehow we talked her into it. It was a long, involved process to convince her it would work. One of her stipulations in saying yes was that I would go along. We got someone to go to her place and fix her hair (she couldn't walk down to ZCMI to her favorite hairdresser anymore) and help her decide what to wear.

On Tuesday, February 26, 1974, Mark, John, Bruce, and Jeff, Aunt Florence's dates, picked her up. A night to be remembered was under way. All the effort of the planning was worth it just for the look on Aunt Florence's face when she first met Bill Howard and Zelmo Beatty, both of whom made quite a fuss over her. Later she said, "When I found out who Bill Howard was, I nearly ate him up!" Bill was extremely kind and gracious to his loyal fan. He even interviewed her at halftime on the radio.

When the team came out to warm up, big Zelmo came running right over to Aunt Florence, shook her hand, and signed her program. "I just couldn't believe my eyes when I saw that big tall handsome 'Z' coming toward me!" she exclaimed.

I kept notes during the game, wanting to capture some of this magical evening forever. "Oh, aren't they geniuses?" "Isn't he quick!" "On some of the road trips Willie hasn't played his regular game, but just look at him tonight. Isn't he a whiz?" "Oh boy, this is fun!" "Oh *no!* They called a foul on our Johnny, didn't they!" "Zelmo has trouble with his knees. They take him out to let him rest. He's the oldest one on the team. Bill calls him 'the old man.'"

Even though she was thrilled at being there, she missed her radio. "Oh, how I wish I could hear Bill," she lamented. "This is the first broadcast I've missed. He just guides me all the way through the game." "I'm wondering who the refs are tonight. There are a couple I resent like the devil." "I can't wait to get the paper tomorrow!" "Wait till I call Sis tomorrow!" "When people find out I was here, they'll say, 'Well, she's still kicking!' Who ever dreamed . . . "

Her four handsome dates seemed to enjoy Aunt Florence as much as the game. When she told them how much fun she was having, one of them remarked, "I'll bet we're having a better time than you are, Florence." She just couldn't imagine why four young men would want to dress up "fit to kill," as she put it, and take an old lady to a game.

Too soon it was over, and one young man got on either side of Aunt Florence and started the long walk back to the car. Aunt Florence was flying high as she told them of her youth and her teaching days. They couldn't believe it when she told them how she had sung the tenor lead, Thaddeus, in *Bohemian Girl*, but she described the opera and even sang parts of her two favorite arias. They laughed at her description of the homemade tuxedo she wore when she sang tenor in the Ogden male chorus.

Mark pulled the car as close as possible to the apartment so Florence wouldn't have to walk as far. Then suddenly John asked if she'd like to go get a Big Mac, and her eyes lit up. As we headed that direction, Jeff asked her if she had liked the game. Florence answered, "I'll never forget this night!" As we got close to our destination, Florence said, "I'll get a Big Mac if you'll let me pay for it." Jeff quickly responded, "Now, Florence, we don't wanna hear any more talk like that out of you. You're on a date!"

The food was purchased, and we all sat down around the same table. Florence took a look at her Big Mac and root beer and laughed. "Great big pig me—here I am with a great big Big Mac. Here's for my health! You boys help me eat it; I can never finish this whole thing." But she did, and she ate the whole order of fries besides.

Aunt Florence told the young men a few of her favorite jokes; she was famous for the jokes she knew and the way she told them. She had the boys laughing constantly. I marveled at the collapse of any generation gap between those high-school seniors and an eighty-one-year-old woman. She told them, "I have a friend who had a stroke, and she can't talk. It'd kill me if I couldn't talk!" They got a kick out of that. She had been talking nonstop the whole evening, and they were loving it.

When the boys took her back to number 29 at the Kimball, Florence couldn't seem to find the right words to tell them thank you. Bruce told her they would be back to have family home evening with her, and John said, "Florence, we're going to remember this night for the rest of our lives." She could hardly speak, but she managed to say that she'd never forget it, either.

After they left she sank in her chair and shook her head. She kept wondering aloud, "Who did all this magic?" She reviewed all that had happened, hardly able to believe that it *had* happened. She had to take a sleeping pill so she could settle down after it was all over. I suppose the only thing that could have made it a more perfect evening would have been for the Stars to win the game. In the months that followed she kept reliving that one wonderful, magical night.

Aunt Florence had a wonderful sense of humor. I can still hear her laugh. She got a big kick out of life, herself, and her surroundings. After she'd had one of her strokes and had a little trouble speaking and getting around, she received a letter calling her to jury duty. She was not pleased. Jury duty was something she had always thought she would enjoy, and she was upset that they had waited to invite her until she was unable to do it. I helped her write her letter of response. She explained her disappointment, for after preparing her whole life for just such an opportunity, watching *Perry Mason* and all the other courtroom shows, by the time they invited her she was no longer able to speak clearly or get around well, so she had to decline.

Finally Florence had to go to a nursing home. It was a

very hard thing to do, but there just wasn't any way to avoid it. She could no longer take care of herself in her little apartment. We kept the apartment for her for a long time, hoping she might rally and be able to return. I stayed there alone several times and missed her so much. It was touching to look around that small, small space and think about all her adventures—about the long and fascinating life of Florence Sperry.

When she was eighty-four, she received a letter inviting her to a sales presentation about condominiums and offering her a free gift: her choice of either a beautiful, twenty-piece set of china or an extra-deluxe chain saw. This was her response (with help from my mother and me):

"Dear Mr. Johnston:

"I just received your marvelous letter about the unique condominiums that you have in Park City and Hawaii. Living as I do in a nursing home, you can imagine how delighted I'd be to live in Park City or Hawaii instead. I don't know how I was lucky enough to get on your mailing list, but what a thrill!

"One thing I'm very excited about is the chain saw. It's just what I need here at the nursing home when we work on crafts. Maybe they'll let me start coming again when they realize I've got such a nice saw; I had to quit going because I wasn't participating. I've missed it.

"Another thing I need to mention is that when you fly me over to Hawaii, I'll have to go first class. I've had several strokes, and I just can't seem to hold my legs together anymore, so I'll need the extra space.

"Thanks again for thinking of me here in the nursing home. I think that's great! Owning something for 'the rest of my life,' as you put it, sounds terrific since I'm only 84!"

We can only imagine what it was like for those who received that letter from Aunt Florence.

Some months after Florence passed away, a letter from the IRS arrived saying she hadn't paid her taxes for 1979. Unless she had reasonable cause for delay, she might be liable for penalties. The letter said, "If you believe you had reasonable cause for filing late and for paying late, please explain. We have enclosed an envelope for your use. Thank you for your cooperation."

There was no way we were not going to respond to that letter. My mother called me the minute she got it. As we worked on the reply, we could almost hear Florence's distinctive, infectious laugh mingled with ours. Under 'I did not file the form because,' we checked the 'Business was closed' box. In the remarks section we wrote:

"Yes, business was closed permanently on June 9, 1980. I'd not had an income for quite some years prior to that because I was in a nursing home. I know it is unusual to be getting a letter from me now that I'm dead, but I didn't want to mess up your records. I know how important they are to you. It was only with very special permission that I was able to send this note from the Other Side. I must say it's a lot more fun here where there aren't any taxes, but despite that I do wish you well in your work. I know a lot of people don't fully appreciate what you do, but now that I've got a new perspective (as they say) I know you work hard. By the way, in case anyone there is interested, everything they say is true—you've got to work there for what you get here, if you know what I mean. Tell the guys in the office to get with it. Thanks again for your inquiry and for providing the envelope." I wish we could have watched and listened when the team at the IRS received that letter.

I can hardly wait to see Aunt Florence again; what a happy reunion that will be. It's hard to estimate the influence of that great soul on my life and the life of our family. I spoke at her funeral, trying to capture some of the essence of a unique and wonderful woman—trying, if inadequately, to pay tribute to dear Aunt Florence. For her life, and Sharmayn's and the little Sunbeam's at the creamery and for the lives of all those who touch us every day, I give thanks. As we sing in hymn number 293, each life that touches ours for good reflects the Lord's love for us.

Chapter 9

ON THE WAY
TO A MIRACLE

I WAS ON INTERSTATE 15 HEADING for Salt Lake City to teach at the Missionary Home early on a Sunday morning when something went wrong with my car. I couldn't steer it properly. I pulled over to the side of the road and got out to inspect. Sure enough, a flat tire. Yikes! I knew how to change tires but wasn't much in the mood to do so in my Sunday clothes and in a hurry to get to my meeting.

Lots of people passed without stopping. Many looked as if they were on their way to important meetings too. Some of them seemed to feel bad for me. The looks on their faces indicated they hoped someone would stop—someone who wasn't on the way to a meeting or an appointment.

And then *they* came toward me—three men in an old truck. They weren't in a hurry. They pulled right over and hopped out to see if they could help. What's more, they made it seem as if they were glad I had a flat tire so they could stop and help. They didn't make me feel stupid or unskilled or any such thing.

As I watched and listened and visited with the men I decided to tell them about all the cars that had passed. One of the men laughed and said, "Oh, those are the church people. They're all on their way to a meeting. It's Sunday. They don't have time to stop and help."

I thought, And we're usually on our way to a meeting where we'll discuss the importance of loving our neighbors as ourselves and doing good to others, and how much we need to serve and help one another. I found myself wondering, hard, how many times I had been too busy to stop and help.

I thanked the men sincerely for their help. I know they weren't the Three Nephites, but they were three very kind and helpful neighbors who not only fixed my tire but helped me learn an important lesson. I'd like to be more like them.

One day the Savior was on his way to a miracle. He was responding to a request from Jairus, the ruler of a synagogue, whose only daughter was dying. The people thronged about Jesus as He went along, and a woman who was ill touched the hem of His garment. He stopped. He responded kindly and lovingly to that needy, seeking soul. He comforted her and healed her, and then He continued to Jairus's home. Someone came toward Him from there to let him know that the daughter had already died. Jesus went to the home anyway and restored her to life (see Luke 8:41–56).

The Savior stopped on his way to a miracle to give attention and help to another in need. He did that many times in His ministry.

In 3 Nephi 17 we read about the visit of the Savior to the Nephites. He had been instructing them and asked that they return to their homes to ponder upon what He had said, ask the Father in His name for understanding, and prepare their minds for His return. He then said, "But now I go unto the Father, and also to show myself unto the lost tribes of Israel" (3 Nephi 17:4).

After Jesus said that, He looked on the people and saw that they were weeping and looking "steadfastly upon him as if they would ask him to tarry a little longer with them" (3 Nephi 17:5). And He did. He stopped, with deep compassion and mercy, and remained with them. He had them bring their sick to Him to be healed. He called their little children to Him; He prayed in such a marvelous way that His words could not be written; He wept with them; He blessed their little children one by one and prayed for them; He instituted the sacrament among them. Marvelous things happened because the Savior stopped and remained with them.

How often have you stopped in the hall at school or church, in the parking lot, on your way to a nap, on a busy day—stopped to answer the phone, to visit a neighbor, to listen to a friend in need, to respond to a prompting of the Spirit? Parents do that over and over and over. So do aunts, uncles, neighbors, big and little sisters and brothers, strangers, bus drivers, store clerks, crossing guards, sports heroes, and many others.

Oh, how we need more Christians like those: people who are willing to stop. We all have so many more opportunities to do good and to be good than we respond to. My parents used to say to me in many situations, "What would Jesus do?" That wasn't always what I wanted to hear (I remember thinking, "I want to know what *Porter Rockwell* would do!"), but it was a lasting lesson for me. What would Jesus do? He would stop. On His way to a miracle, a meeting, an appointment, He would—and did—stop.

Once we have an opportunity to stop, it's too late to try to find some instruction book or to attend a seminar on how to respond. What and who we are is what is needed. No manual or handbook can tell us how to respond in those moments when one individual needs us and we have a chance to help. We need to get ready ahead of time. We can prepare spiritually by learning what's in the Lord's "handbook" and practicing working with the Spirit. We can all become better at responding to those sweet, still, small promptings.

During 1993, a wonderful companion with whom I served in Indonesia came to America to attend the temple and visit some people she had known in Indonesia. Her name is Endang (rhymes with *song* rather than *sang*). She had saved and waited for a long, long time—nearly twenty years—for this chance to come to the temple. It was her first trip away from her own country, and almost everything was new to her.

Endang first went to Arizona to stay with the Wadsworths, a couple she had helped by interpreting for them when they were serving in Indonesia. She went to the Mesa Temple again and again. She did work for her mother and others in her family in addition to receiving her own endowment. She said that when she was able to go through the ceremony without any help, the temple workers cried. They had become accustomed to seeing her there day after day.

She came to Provo by way of other places and other temples, and I had the privilege of spending some time with her. We went to the Provo Temple, the eighth one she had been in during her time in America. We sat in the celestial room and cried, both of us wanting so much to live so that we can sit down together in the celestial kingdom together someday. Lucy Mack Smith said something tender about that at an early Relief Society meeting in Nauvoo: "We must cherish one another, watch over one another, comfort one another, and give instructions that we may all sit down in heaven together."

Endang went with me to sisters' meeting one Sunday at the Missionary Training Center, and I invited her to offer the opening prayer (in Indonesian) and then share her testimony. How tender and wonderful her words were. She spoke of this being her first time in America and what a big decision it was to come. She explained that she didn't even know how to use a telephone or get water from a tap. Yet she felt Heavenly Father helping her. What a blessing it was to be with her and to relive so many memories of our time together. She is currently teaching seminary and institute classes in Solo, Central Java.

Endang and I had an extraordinary experience while we were touring the Relief Society building with Nan and Joy, two other friends who had also served as missionaries in Indonesia. I knew that the Primary presidency and general board were having a meeting, and I hesitated for a moment to interrupt them. But I kept thinking what a blessing it would be for Endang to meet them and for them to meet her. So I took courage and tapped on the door.

They welcomed us instantly, and President Michaelene P. Grassli got up immediately and hugged Endang tight. When Endang realized this was the president of the Primary for the whole Church she just kept gasping and exclaiming, "Oh my! Oh my goodness!" They all sang the "Hello" song to her and then "I Love to See the Temple."

I learned a great, important lesson from that experience. Those women weren't just talking about being kind and reaching the one—they *did* it. They stopped what they were doing and showed that people really do matter more than meetings. Later it occurred to me that they could easily have said something like, "I'm sorry, we just don't have time right now. We're having this important meeting on how important it is to help Heavenly Father's children. Sorry." I'm grateful for the lesson they taught through their example of stopping and focusing on what and who mattered most—in this instance, Endang.

When I think of people stopping, I often think of parents

and others who stop to help little children. They often deny themselves quiet time, privacy, and personal projects because a child needs them. They'll read the same story, watch the same video, look at the same cloud, examine the same grasshopper, over and over again. Some of those stops create more precious memories than the quiet, private time would have. Seldom have I heard an "if only" like "If only I had cleaned the bathroom that day" or "If only I had finished that book I was reading." I *have* heard and felt the sorrow of "If only I had listened to him" and "If only I'd taken time to go with her." Relationships, people, are what matter most.

Several years ago I received a prompting to visit my neighbor Val. She had cancer and wasn't doing very well. I resisted. I let the still small voice know how busy I was. Thank goodness the prompting continued until I finally responded and stopped on my way home one evening. I told Val honestly that I came by because I was in the neighbor-hood—she and Mac lived just up the street from me. What a great time we had talking and laughing. I came away feeling renewed and wondering why I hadn't stopped sooner.

As the weeks and months went by, I visited Val regularly and we became good friends. She worked for a while at the MTC, where I also was working. She was in the bookstore and became a good friend to many missionaries. She did extra things for them and helped them overcome their homesickness and get adjusted to life in the MTC. She had a wonderful combination of kindness and humor.

When Val was told that her cancer had invaded her liver and she had only about three more months to live, she decided she was not ready for such news—she had a few more things to accomplish with her family. She decided that doctors were doctors, but Val was Val. And she made it. She lived many months longer than predicted and accomplished some wonderful things. I remember the day we talked about her making a tape for her husband and children. My cousin Ida had died of cancer, leaving six children, and had made a taped message for each of them. Val did something similar and told me it was a very tender, meaningful experience.

She had extraordinary help and support from her husband, Mac, and the rest of her family, as well as from several neighbors who gave much time and care. Her last months were not easy. They were filled with pain and suffering and many unanswered questions.

On the Wednesday before she died, I made my last visit to Val. She asked me an interesting question: "How do I get There from here?" We had talked many times about death and the life afterward, so the question didn't surprise me. I felt happy for having had some experience with death during the years I worked as a nurse. I was able to answer her honestly with what I felt was one of the most comforting, kind things God provides for us: "Someone will come to meet you—someone you love and trust. That person will show you what to do and where to go. You won't be afraid." She told me she didn't know it would be so hard to die—so hard to get from here to There.

Several days later Val passed away, and I was asked to speak at her funeral. I had a hard time expressing how much she had helped me learn and understand about life and death. I thought of a verse from the Doctrine and Covenants: "And there shall be silence in heaven for the space of half an hour; and immediately after shall the curtain of heaven be unfolded, as a scroll is unfolded after it is rolled up, and the face of the Lord shall be unveiled" (D&C 88:95). I wondered what I would think about in that last half hour when it would be all finished—no more chance to work, to serve, to repent, to put first things first.

I thought about Val as she got ready to go Home. She was

thinking about her family: her husband, her children, her mother, her sister. She was thinking about Heavenly Father and the Savior and those waiting for her in another place. She was bringing back happy memories of time she had spent doing things that mattered most. I can't adequately express my thanks to Heavenly Father for the prompting to stop and learn from Val.

As we strive to become more like the Savior, we will feel closer to Him and more aware of His influence in our lives and the lives of others. For a few months of my life I lived in Nigeria, West Africa. In our branch was a precious little child whom I called Broomstick; she was seven years old and weighed all of twenty-three pounds. Often when I entered the small place we had rented to use as our chapel she would be sitting on the back bench. I loved to pick her up and take her to the front with me and hold her during the meetings. She would soak up all the love that I had in me and more—but it was always replaced and increased.

Once at Easter time I was holding my little friend when it was announced that we would sing hymn number 136, "I Know That My Redeemer Lives." I felt prompted to sing it to her. It was a powerful, sweet, unforgettable experience for me, and maybe for her as well. Those words were so meaningful and touching: "I know that your Redeemer lives. What comfort this sweet sentence gives! He lives to bless you with His love. He lives to plead for you above. He lives, your hungry soul to feed. He lives to bless in time of need. . . . He lives to comfort you when faint. He lives to hear your soul's complaint. He lives to silence all your fears. He lives to wipe away your tears. He lives to calm your troubled heart. He lives all blessings to impart. He lives, your kind, wise, heav'nly Friend. He lives and loves you to the end. . . . He lives and grants you daily breath. He lives, and you shall conquer death. He lives your mansion to prepare. He lives to bring you safely there."

That experience had an enormous effect on me. I realized that Christ does *for each one of us* all the things mentioned in that hymn and that He needs us to participate in the stopping and the doing.

At one point in my life, a certain phrase I included in my prayers had become so familiar that it came out rapidly and with almost no meaning. It went something like this: "Bless the poor and the needy, the sick and the afflicted, and those that have cause to mourn." I would almost add, "And good luck!" It didn't occur to me that perhaps I should offer to be on the team, willing to participate in the miracle of serving, comforting, and healing. Was I becoming a "minimal Mormon," a "not-quite Christian"?

I came to recognize that many of my own prayers and pleadings had been answered through other people. That's a wise plan—a plan in which we need each other, in which we are interdependent. Both those who give and those who receive are thereby blessed and come closer to their divine potential.

As President Marion G. Romney said, "There is an interdependence between those who have and those who have not. The process of giving exalts the poor and humbles the rich. In the process, both are sanctified" (*Ensign*, Nov. 1982, p. 93).

Leo Tolstoy put it this way: "I know that God does not desire men to live apart from each other, and therefore has not revealed to them what is needful for each of them to live by himself. He wishes them to live together, united, and therefore has revealed to them that they are needful to each other's happiness. I know now that people only seem to live when they care only for themselves, and that it is by love for others that they really live. He who has love has God in him, and is in God—because God is love."

And that great soul Helen Keller said: "I believe that love will finally establish the kingdom of God on earth, and that cornerstones of that kingdom will be liberty, truth, brotherhood, and service. I believe that we can live on earth according to the fulfillment of God's will, and that when the will of God is done on earth as it is in heaven, every man will love his fellow men and act toward them as he desires they should act toward him. I believe that the welfare of each is bound up in the welfare of all" (*The Faith of Helen Keller* [Kansas City, Missouri: Hallmark, 1967], p. 32).

A greeting used in Africa impresses me. One person will ask of another, "Are you well?" The response is, "I am well if you are well." It is as if they have a deep, sweet understanding of the apostle Paul's teachings in the twelfth chapter of 1 Corinthians. He teaches that we are one body with many members and that we have great and continuing need for each other—with all our variety, our strengths, our needs, our love, and our experience. And we do have great need of those "which seem to be more feeble"; they are necessary to our wholeness and our progression. "And whether one member suffer, all the members suffer with it; or one member be honoured, all the members rejoice with it" (1 Corinthians 12:26). The Savior has taught us to be one and to consider each one. We are to esteem others as ourselves (see D&C 38:24–27) and to love others as He does. Is there a better way to become more like Him?

We are needed to help prepare for the Savior to come again; we need to be prepared individually and also as a people, as a society. What are we willing to do? That's where we start: we are willing. Willing to stop on our way to a miracle, a movie, a meeting. Willing to bear one another's burdens that they may be light, to mourn with those that mourn and comfort those who stand in need of comfort. Willing to take upon us the name of Christ—to be known by and called by and worthy of such a holy, sacred name (see Mosiah 18:8–11). We are covenant people.

There are so many big and little things we can do that will increase our love, compassion, and responsiveness to the Spirit. Some of the following suggestions may be helpful:

—Visit someone who can't come to see you. The Savior used the word *visit* many times and also taught that great principle by example.

—Think of reasons why people do and say the things they do, especially if there are things you don't readily understand.

—Strive to avoid reacting to others in negative, angry ways.

—Practice becoming a better listener; pay attention and go beyond hearing the words to gaining understanding.

—Once a week, speak to someone whom you don't know (yet).

—Work to develop a countenance of love; strive to look at others in such a way that they know they are loved even if they have no idea who you are.

—Remember that your own sorrows and challenges can deepen your compassion and patience.

—Minimize any competition you feel toward anyone else; cooperation rather than competition will accomplish much good.

—Rejoice in the success and accomplishments of others rather than feeling envy or jealousy.

—Make it a point to relate to and associate with children and older friends often; they can share important lessons about how to be childlike and genuine.

—Seek promptings to contact someone in need; exercise

the capacity to be responsive to the Spirit and to become a more effective instrument in God's hands.

—Cheerfully and willingly respond to opportunities for service even when it's inconvenient and may require sacrifice.

—Sit in a busy place once or twice a year and watch the people: their faces, their nonverbal messages, their interaction with others. Try to imagine what their challenges and burdens might be, along with their happiness.

—See if you can find someone who has a need to give, and think of something that person can do for you or teach you.

—Live more fully the law of the fast as explained so beautifully in Isaiah 58:5–12.

—Appreciate more than you expect; gratitude is an attitude.

—Think of someone specific whom you need to telephone or write a note to; decide when you will do it— within the week, on Sunday, whatever. Then stick to your decision: *do it!*

—Be specific in your prayers; pray about individuals who come into your heart and mind as you are communicating with your Heavenly Father. Ask Him if there is anything He needs to have you do. "Feast upon the words of Christ; for behold, the words of Christ will tell you all things what ye should do" (2 Nephi 32:3).

Can we comprehend what it might be like to be invited to sit on the right hand of God at some future day because we truly fed the hungry, clothed the naked, visited the sick, and administered to their relief, "both spiritually and temporally, according to their wants"? (see Matthew 25:34–40; Mosiah 4:26). May our awareness of the Savior and those for whom He suffered and died cause us to be willing to serve Him by serving others. May we come unto Jesus with broken hearts and contrite spirits, ready to participate in the needed miracles. May we ever be ready to "succor the weak, lift up the hands which hang down, and strengthen the feeble knees" (D&C 81:5). May those who are strong be willing to help those who are weak (see Romans 15:1). May we be willing to stop and do what we can to help, even when we're on the way to a miracle.

Chapter 10

MAGNIFYING
OUR TALENTS

Sure, I took piano lessons. Didn't everyone? I hated practicing; I wanted just to play. But Mrs. Jones was quite insistent about all the scales and arpeggios, and my parents backed her up—she was, after all, one of the best piano teachers in town. So I practiced, but not often with great, swelling feelings of joy.

I always thought that magnifying talents meant you practiced and practiced until you got really good at something—so good you could show off. If you magnified your piano talent, you would soon play so well that people would be jealous of you, and your mother could leave the door open when you practiced—not the door of the living room where the piano was, but the front door. Then everyone in the neighborhood would be able to hear, and they'd be amazed and thrilled. Probably they'd come and crowd onto the front lawn just to listen to your practicing because you were so good.

Mom and Dad never were able to leave the front door open when I practiced. Alan Seegmiller's parents could and did, and I remember hearing him play and wondering how in the world he could make his fingers do all that stuff. My parents weren't able to leave the front door open until my brother Richard came along. He was the last of the eight of us, and for some reason it "took" for him. He was playing Big Stuff—the fourteen-page, hubba-hubba things—and playing it well. I used to ask him to play for my friends whenever they came over. He could play without even looking at the book. And Mom left the front door open.

Anyway, I thought magnifying talents was a very focused-on-yourself kind of thing. You got better and better and people began to notice and they asked you to play at funerals and weddings and the openings of new stores. You would accompany people who sang or played the violin, but you could also do solo numbers. Maybe you'd even get to a point where you'd charge someone two dollars to have you come and play for an event.

Sometimes I imagined myself as a person who had magnified her talents and was now approaching The Judgment Bar, having passed away in the prime of life. At some check-in point I am asked if I have magnified my talents. "Of course!" I reply. "Surely you've heard of me." Then they ask if I would like to show them. Certainly. This is no big deal. I've been showing off my whole life. They roll out the golden heavenly grand piano. I ask all the angels or whoever is there to please be quiet and respectful. And away I go. A concert for the ages. I bring everyone to tears! They welcome me in with great enthusiasm.

I have since learned that magnifying talents means something quite different. It is illustrated by a woman I met once who had taught more than two hundred piano students. Maybe that's not a record, but it's extremely impressive and in itself should assure her sainthood. Now, think of her at some check-in point in a few years. "Did you magnify your talents?" they ask, and she replies in a genuine, humble way,

101

"I really worked at it." "Would you like to show us?" "You mean here and now?" "Yes, please." "All right." So they roll out two hundred golden heavenly grand pianos, and all those whom she has taught and helped are playing, and she's just sitting on a lawn chair eating grapes.

Part of magnifying talents is giving them away, investing in others and allowing them to be successful. It includes not being threatened by the fact that eventually someone you have taught will play the piano or do something else better than you can.

The Doctrine and Covenants teaches this wonderful truth about magnifying talents: "And you are to be equal, or in other words, you are to have equal claims on the properties, for the benefit of managing the concerns of your stewardships, every man according to his wants and his needs, inasmuch as his wants are just—and all this for the benefit of the church of the living God, that every man may improve upon his talent, that every man may gain other talents, yea, even an hundred fold, to be cast into the Lord's storehouse, to become the common property of the whole church—every man seeking the interest of his neighbor, and doing all things with an eye single to the glory of God" (D&C 82:17–19).

We gain talents and magnify them in order that we might be of use to God's children. When I read those verses I think of the "yea" as a "yippee yea," a celebration of the willingness of those who have to share with those in need. There's a feeling of hooray about the idea of every person being willing to share with others, to help with an eye single to the glory of God, which is to bring to pass the immortality and eternal life of man (see Moses 1:39).

The idea of magnifying talents takes me back to my childhood, when I would sit on the back porch with my little plastic magnifying glass. I could see things through that glass that I couldn't see with my naked eye. I loved looking at my hands and dirt and leaves and grasshoppers—anything that would hold still long enough—and seeing them in a different way than usual. That makes me wonder: Can God see in us things we can't see with our naked, natural eye? When He speaks of magnifying us, is part of that His ability to find talents in us that we don't know we have? Does He give us experiences that help us increase and magnify our talents so that we have more to share?

Many of our most important talents, which we seek to magnify in order to be of greater service, have nothing to do with pianos and violins and needles (those that sew or those that deliver medicine, depending on the need). The hymn "More Holiness Give Me" lists some of those greater talents, things like humility and empathy, meekness and patience, trust and joy, praise and purpose (see *Hymns*, no. 131). The phrases in the hymn are like a menu of ingredients in our quest to come closer to Christ and become more like Him.

As Moroni was finishing his record he invited us to seek for more holiness. "Yea, come unto Christ, and be perfected in him, and deny yourselves of all ungodliness; and if ye shall deny yourselves of all ungodliness, and love God with all your might, mind and strength, then is his grace sufficient for you, that by his grace ye may be perfect in Christ; and if by the grace of God ye are perfect in Christ, ye can in nowise deny the power of God" (Moroni 10:32). What does it mean to deny ourselves of all ungodliness? That could take a while. It feels like it could take forever when I think of my weaknesses and all the ways in which I want to become holier.

I've long believed that the closer we come to Christ, the more aware we are of what we yet lack in becoming like Him. At the same time, the closer we are, the more we can allow Him to help us become more perfect—more whole and complete, healed and pure. We become more able to have tears for His sorrows and pain at His grief—and to feel what causes Him sorrow and grief. We have more meekness in suffering and more praise for relief. We are increasingly aware of what He notices, what He feels, what He would have us do.

As we come closer to Christ, we respond better to the Spirit, the still small voice. We become more receptive to promptings from a Source who has an eternal view of things and knows how we can fit in and help. For we *can* help in significant ways, and in little, quiet ways, to rescue each other. The fact of our interdependence—our need for each other—is to me one of the most compelling realities in life.

Galatians 5:22–23 offers some descriptions of how the Spirit works, what kind of feelings come to us: "The fruit of the Spirit is love, joy, peace, longsuffering, gentleness, goodness, faith, meekness, temperance."

I also appreciate the description in Doctrine and Covenants 11:10–14: "Behold, thou hast a gift, or thou shalt have a gift if thou wilt desire of me in faith, with an honest heart, believing in the power of Jesus Christ, or in my power which speaketh unto thee;

"For, behold, it is I that speak; behold, I am the light which shineth in darkness, and by my power I give these words unto thee.

"And now, verily, verily, I say unto thee, put your trust in that Spirit which leadeth to do good—yea, to do justly, to walk humbly, to judge righteously; and this is my Spirit.

"Verily, verily, I say unto you, I will impart unto you of my Spirit, which shall enlighten your mind, which shall fill your soul with joy;

"And then shall ye know, or by this shall you know, all things whatsoever you desire of me, which are pertaining unto things of righteousness, in faith believing in me that you shall receive."

How often have we felt like this: More promptings from the Spirit, yes—when it's a little more convenient. More holiness, yes—but not if I have to make major changes in my life. More patience in suffering, yes—but not too much suffering, and not until I indicate that I'm ready for it, please. I have asked many times in my life, "Why me?" And I ask it usually when I'm having a hard time—not nearly often enough when I've been blessed with relief. I want to have more faith in my Savior, yes, and more trust in the Lord, but do I really have to trust him with *everything*? It's a fact of life that we can't have more Y without more X. There are prices for everything, laws upon which all blessings are based (see D&C 130:20–21.)

Do I want an abundance of roses without more thorns? Leisure without work? Dessert without vegetables? More strawberries without more weeds? The ability to magnify talents, from piano to patience, from violin to virtue, without expending any effort? Do I count the cost? Am I willing to pay the price? Athletes don't seem to be able to decide a week ahead that they're going to participate in the Olympics. They spend a lifetime of hard work preparing, and the practices are seldom carried out with cheering crowds all around.

In nursing classes we learned about the "disuse phenomenon": That which we don't use diminishes in size and usefulness. One powerful example of that was when I wore a cast on my leg for a couple of months. When the cast came off, I was shocked at the skinny, hairy leg that dangled from my body. I wasn't able just to jump up and run and leap tall buildings in a single bound. The muscles had visibly diminished in size, and it was quickly apparent that they had also diminished in usefulness. It took time, exercise, and a lot of patience to get my leg back to where it had been.

Maybe if we don't exercise virtue and holiness and faith and trust and love, those talents shrink in size or usefulness. The other side of the disuse phenomenon is also true; maybe we could call it the "use phenomenon": That which we use increases in size and usefulness. Wear your muscles out with strenuous exercise and they will grow big and hard. Go barefooted for a few months over rough terrain, and the soles of your feet will become tough and durable. I'm convinced that this law is operative not just with muscles but with our ability to serve, to love, to have purpose in prayer and more sense of His care.

Someone once shared with me a fascinating story of an ancient Roman aqueduct in Spain. For eighteen hundred years this aqueduct had carried the cool waters of the Rio Frio down from the high mountains to the thirsty city. Nearly sixty generations of men drank from it. Then came another generation, which said, "This aqueduct is so great a marvel that it should be preserved for our children. We will relieve it of its centuries-old labors." So they laid modern pipelines to give it a reverent rest. Soon the aqueduct began to fall apart. Built originally of rough-hewn granite blocks, without lime or cement, the sediment of centuries had formed a natural mortar. Now the sun dried it out, and it began to crumble and fall apart. What centuries of service could not destroy, idleness disintegrated.

That story illustrates powerfully why we should be anxiously engaged in good causes and seeking to increase our ability to work with and respond to spiritual promptings. Truly our lives are prolonged and saved through service. I remember hearing Elder Vaughn J. Featherstone repeat a profound thought: "In the days of service, all things are founded; in the days of privilege, all things deteriorate; in the days of vanity, all things are lost."

Gifts and talents that we don't use and share seem to diminish. It seems true that the more we serve, the more we are able to serve. Our service muscles increase in size and usefulness. The use phenomenon is a lot like the law of the harvest: We reap what we sow. We can't pick a tomato or a carrot if we never planted and cared for a seed. We can't expect to become more holy if we never plant the seeds of spirituality.

In some ways, the search for more holiness is an invitation to become more peculiar. Many of the qualities and talents that are magnified in us cause us to be increasingly *unworldly.* We're different in good and happy ways. We stand out. The dictionary defines *peculiar* as "that which pertains to or characterizes an individual person, place or thing, or group of persons or things, as distinct from others; set apart; distinguished in nature, character, or attributes from others; unlike others, singular, uncommon, unusual." Try applying that definition to Deuteronomy 14:2, "For thou art an holy people unto the Lord thy God, and the Lord hath chosen thee to be a peculiar people unto himself." The apostle Peter said it this way: "But ye are a chosen generation, a royal priesthood, an holy nation, a peculiar people; that ye should shew forth the praises of him who hath called you out of darkness into his marvellous light" (1 Peter 2:9). The Lord's people are holy and peculiar, set apart, magnified in doing good and being good.

Suppose I don't know you but I want to. What would I learn about you if I visited your home? What is hanging on the walls? What books and magazines would I notice? What's playing on the TV set? Is there anything "peculiar" about the way you dress or the way you talk? What would I learn about you if I knew how you spent your money and your time? What if I observed your relationships with others? What is being magnified in your life? What is peculiar about you?

Does it make us uncomfortable to be peculiar? Some people struggle to their last minute and penny and breath to look like, behave like, talk like, and become like everyone else. They want to blend in, not to stand out or stand up. They seek to magnify talents not to help bring to pass the immortality and eternal life of God's children but to increase their own magnificence.

It seems, doesn't it, that the gulf between being peculiar (righteous and holy and good) and being like everyone else is getting wider. There is an increasing gulf between good and bad and even between good and better. There are many shades of gray, yes, but there's also still white. Alma 5:57 advises us to "come ye out from the wicked, and be ye separate."

We are a peculiar, covenant people, and almost every week we say *amen* to the following phrase: "That [we] may always have his Spirit to be with [us]." Does it happen? What does the Spirit do? How does the still small voice communicate with us? Are there things we can do to increase our sensitivity to that voice? The Spirit can help us to know what Jesus would do in any situation as well as what He would have *us* do.

The effects of the Spirit and the Lord's guidance are beautifully expressed in another of my favorite hymns, "Let the Holy Spirit Guide" (*Hymns*, no. 143):

> *Let the Holy Spirit guide;*
> *Let him teach us what is true.*
> *He will testify of Christ,*
> *Light our minds with heaven's view.*
>
> *Let the Holy Spirit guard;*
> *Let his whisper govern choice.*

He will lead us safely home
If we listen to his voice.

Let the Spirit heal our hearts
Thru his quiet, gentle pow'r.
May we purify our lives
To receive him hour by hour.

I'm convinced that no power on earth can separate us from God's love and light if we choose to come unto Christ and stay. God's gifts are constant. So is the price. There is never a sale, nor does the price ever go up. He will help us magnify what we can do to help Him in his holy, critical work of saving and rescuing God's children and helping them to go back Home. God helps those who help themselves—but He also helps those who can't help themselves (and sometimes that's me, and sometimes that's you).

Part of God's will for us is that we help to bring to the world peace and hope and rest—rest from suffering, from fear, from doubt and ignorance, from hopelessness and helplessness. The scriptures are full of tender promises regarding that rest:

"They that sow in tears shall reap in joy" (Psalm 126:5).

"And it shall be said in that day, Lo, this is our God; we have waited for him, and he will save us: this is the Lord; we have waited for him, we will be glad and rejoice in his salvation" (Isaiah 25:8–9).

"And God shall wipe away all tears from their eyes; and there shall be no more death, neither sorrow, nor crying, neither shall there be any more pain: for the former things are passed away" (Revelation 21:4).

"Blessed are ye that hunger now: for ye shall be filled. Blessed are ye that weep now: for ye shall laugh" (Luke 6:21).

Jesus has more than enough power and love and experience to understand, succor, comfort, sanctify, rescue, heal, bless, and save. He is our Brother, our Everlasting Friend, our Savior, King, and Redeemer, our Prince of Peace and Good Shepherd. And He is kind and patient and merciful enough to let us help, even in our weakness and despite our feelings of inadequacy. He will help us turn our weaknesses into strengths and magnify the talents and gifts He has so kindly shared with us, in order that we might be more useful in His work.

Chapter 11

ARE WE NOT ALL REFUGEES?

SOMETIMES I ACCIDENTALLY watch the news, and it makes me sad and sick to know of the suffering and struggling of so many of Heavenly Father's children. I'm dismayed and troubled by all the millions who don't have anyone to let them know they have a Savior and Redeemer and where and how to make contact with Him. The world is an unsafe place for many.

The concept of safety, of refuge, of sanctuary has become increasingly important to me through the years and experiences of my life. We sing about it in "How Firm a Foundation" (*Hymns*, no. 85): "Who unto the Savior for refuge have fled." I suppose in some sense everyone who seeks a refuge is a refugee. There have been many in history—individuals and families and whole groups of people. Jesus went with His parents to Egypt. Abraham left Ur of the Chaldees. Lehi took his family into the wilderness and eventually across the ocean. Jared and his brother did the same. The pioneers left their homes and walked across the plains. All around us are examples of the search for a refuge, a safe place.

Early in 1994 I stopped by the visitors center in Mesa,

Arizona, early on a Sunday morning to see the sister missionaries I had met in the Missionary Training Center. We had a joyous reunion, and I enjoyed finding out how they were and what their work was like. As we were visiting, a man came through the front door. No one else was around on that quiet Sunday morning, so he really stood out. He looked as if he hadn't had a chance to bathe, eat, shave, or rest for a while.

I watched as one of the young sister missionaries went over to him. She smiled and greeted him with genuine good feelings. "Good morning!" she said, shaking his hand. "May we help you?" He said somewhat hesitantly that he was new in the area and wondered where a man might get a bite to eat and some kind of help. Instantly she responded with kindness and sincerity, "You've come to the right place!" She went on to tell him where he could get some help; apparently there was a shelter nearby. I'll always remember her wonderful response to someone in need, "You've come to the right place!"

So many of Heavenly Father's children are in need of rescue—in need of a shelter, a safe place, a refuge. They need some haven where they can rest and be free from the trouble that has seemed to surround them. If we as Saints do not provide that refuge, where will such people go?

It seems to me that much of what we do to serve and help others is connected to instruction from the Savior in Matthew 25:34–40. He explained that He was hungry, thirsty, sick, imprisoned, a stranger, naked, and so on, and those called to be on His right hand had responded; they had done what they could to help. And inasmuch as they had served the "least of these" it was as if the service had been given to Him. What a tender, holy, awesome thought.

I looked up the definitions of the words Jesus chose to describe His distress and found that they have broad meaning. In fact, there are chances all around us every day to rescue and save and provide refuge for others. We don't have to travel to another country or be part of a project to respond to the Savior's admonition. Here are some of the meanings I discovered:

Hungry: Any degree of needing or wanting; any strong desire. To crave something eagerly, including such things as attention, love, caring, hope, comfort.

Thirsty: The distressful feeling caused by a desire or need for water or other drink. A strong desire, craving, longing.

Stranger: Outsider, newcomer, foreigner; a person unknown or unfamiliar to one.

Naked: Uncovered, exposed, lacking clothing or means of support; destitute. Without protection or defense. Lacking a necessary condition.

Sick: In poor health, weak, not having well-being, deeply disturbed or distressed. Extremely upset, as by grief, disappointment, failure, and so on. Having a great longing for.

Imprisoned: Restricted, limited, or confined in any way.

To be deprived of love, attention, hope, comfort, and caring is perhaps the worst kind of hunger or thirst. Our rescuing response may not always be to provide food or drink but perhaps to offer time and watch-care, to bear one another's burdens, to comfort each other, to mourn together (see Mosiah 18:8–11.) For the naked, for those who are vulnerable and without protection, we might clothe them not just with a shirt or shoes but with friendship and kindness, with unconditional love. For those who are new, whom we don't know, we can help them to become fellowcitizens so they no longer need to feel like strangers and foreigners (see Ephesians 2:19). We can respond as Christ would—or as we would respond to Christ—to those who are sick, weakened and helpless and distressed, without family or food, home or country, rest or peace.

In 1981 I was in a place called Phanatnikom, a refugee camp in Thailand where survivors of the terrors in other Southeast Asian countries had fled for safety. I was visiting a group of outstanding sister missionaries who were serving the people of the camp. We celebrated the Fourth of July on Saturday by going to a nearby park and playing all kinds of games with little children. We couldn't speak to each other in words, but we did communicate and have a very happy time.

We then visited the places where the sisters were living: the pig farm and the duck farm, about two miles apart. At the pig farm we had an American lunch of chicken, fruit salad, potato salad, and some cookies with genuine chocolate chips that had recently arrived through the mail. Then we began our fast in preparation for fast Sunday, July 5. I recognized that in an extremely minor way I would be experiencing something most of these people had gone through day after day—the feeling of being hungry and thirsty. It also occurred to me that the next day was the Fourth of July in America, and here I was surrounded by people who had been through tremendous terror and sacrifice in their search for freedom, for refuge, for safety.

Sunday morning as we got close to the camp I felt a deep, tangible feeling of anticipation. It's hard to describe, but I knew that I would be there only once for the first time; only once would I feel that first impression of this refugee camp. I also felt that after I visited the camp I would never feel or be the same. That turned out to be more true than I could have imagined.

There were two camps in Phanatnikom. One was a holding camp, a huge area crammed with buildings where the refugees were stashed. They had no idea when they would go to a new country and begin to make a home and a life again. They lived each day trying to keep up their hope, but trying not to hope *too* much, and working to be patient in their difficult circumstances. On the other side of the road was a transit camp, whose inhabitants were just waiting for their sponsorship or their name to be called to go to their third country. Some of them would go to Bataan in the Philippines to wait to go to their fourth country.

Our first stop as we entered the camp was the office of WSURT, Welfare Services Unit for Refugees in Thailand. That was what the Latter-day Saint group was called. The office was not very big, but it was extremely important. It contained the materials and visual aids the missionaries used to help the people get ready for life in another culture, another land. Because many of the refugees would be going to the United States, many of the lessons were based on the culture and living conditions there.

The missionaries had also done things in the camp to give it more feeling of community. All the buildings and areas had been numbered, but on the recommendation of the missionaries the "streets" had also been named. Signs proclaimed "Main Street" and the like.

The homes in which the people lived were built in quad fashion of four buildings facing each other. Each building had three sections, and each section housed a family. The sections were about eight by sixteen feet, if that big. None of the sections had four walls; each family was given twenty pieces of bamboo to finish off the fourth. Loudspeakers in the camp blasted announcements and information almost constantly. The sisters had to teach above that noise.

A water truck came around every few days and pumped water into receptacles from which the people would draw their own water supply. Water was a precious commodity, as it is in most of the world. The people used buckets or what-ever they had to haul the amount they were allowed back to their homes. With this small allowance of water they cooked, bathed, washed their clothing, and so on. No wonder when the rain came and poured off the roofs they ran to bathe and wash their hair.

I loved watching the smiles and enthusiasm with which the people greeted our great missionaries as they mingled with them in the camp. These remarkable women accomplished miracles every day. As they shared their experiences I became increasingly aware of their devotion, their love for the refugees, their personal sacrifices, their willingness to give and give and give, day after day. I watched them with the people and with each other, serving with a marvelous unity in their diversity. I observed many unselfish, spontaneous acts of service and kindness in my time with them. I came away with a deep respect and admiration for them and what they had accomplished. In no way do I pretend to have experienced even a small part of what they went through in the months they served and worked in the camps. But what little I experienced personally has permanently changed my life.

One of the first people I met, besides the remarkable women and one couple who were serving there as missionaries, was Trach Khuong, one of the translators for the sisters. He held a book on which was printed on the outside: "This book belongs to Trach Khuong, a member of The Church of Jesus Christ of Latter-day Saints." He had been baptized about ten years earlier in the United States but had returned to Vietnam and hadn't had much contact with the Church until he ended up in the camp in Thailand and met the sister missionaries. He spoke Vietnamese, English, and Khmer, and he was a great help to the work of the WSURT team. I was told that without him it would have been impossible to hold church services in the camp, because the refugees had to be the ones to lead any religious services.

We had our church service in what was called the "Model

Home." This place was a dream come true for the sisters, who had wanted to fix up a place where they could show the people what a house was like in other parts of the world. They were told they could fix up the Model Home as long as they didn't use any of the money from the WSURT program. So they scrounged around for whatever they could find. One day they received twenty-five dollars from a woman in Provo who said she had extra and wanted to share it. She had sent the check to the camp through Elder Marion D. Hanks, who was responsible for getting that wonderful work started in Southeast Asia.

The sisters cashed the check and used it for paint for the walls in the three or four sections they had designated as different rooms in this one building. They found pictures to hang on the walls. The missionary couple, the Andersons, delivered an old, wrecked refrigerator, and the sisters found an old stove and counter. They had a sink propped up on some boards, and a toilet. None of the appliances was hooked up, but at least the sisters were able to show the people what different rooms in a home might look like.

This, then, was where we had our sacrament meeting, in the Model Home, sitting in a circle on little stools. Twenty-two people attended, including the missionaries, the Andersons, Khuong, and several refugees who were not members of the Church. There was no piano or organ or pulpit or anything, but oh! there was a spirit of peace and a closeness to each other.

We hummed and sang the prelude music, "A Poor Wayfaring Man of Grief." The words had particular power and meaning in that setting. For our opening hymn we sang "Dearest Children, God Is Near You," and as I observed the many who were outside looking in, I felt that the words were certainly for them. God *is* near you. He knows what you've been through, little boy wearing a Pizza Hut hat. He knows where you are. Please know that somehow.

We sang a sacrament hymn and then Khuong blessed the bread and Elder Anderson passed it. Then Elder Anderson blessed the water and Khuong passed it. We sang "How Firm a Foundation" (the words were still "You who unto Jesus for refuge have fled"), and I was deeply touched as we sang those words in those circumstances. The refugees had indeed come to Jesus for refuge, for a haven and a protection from the terrible experiences they had suffered, for a perfect brightness of hope. All the words from that hymn seemed to have greater meaning in such a place:

In ev'ry condition—in sickness, in health,
In poverty's vale or abounding in wealth
At home or abroad, on the land or the sea—. . .
As thy days may demand, so thy succor shall be.

When I sing hymn number 85 now, I think of Phanatnikom.

Khuong began the testimony meeting by sharing his own testimony. He started, "We have a lot in common." What a good shepherd this group leader was. He spoke first in English and then switched to Vietnamese so others could understand what he was saying. Some of the sisters shared their testimonies, including Rita, the director of the program in the camp, who had been there from the beginning and had served for nearly ten months. This was her last Sunday there. Elder Anderson shared his feelings, mentioning that many Southeast Asians who had joined the Church in other lands had done so because of the influence of the welfare missionaries who had to teach by who they were— by their example—because they were not allowed to preach.

For our closing hymn we sang "Come unto Jesus" (*Hymns*, no. 117). I was very emotional about that hymn. Not only is it one of my favorite hymns but it seemed perfect to sing in that particular time and place. Here we were, from several different lands, joining our hearts and our voices and our feelings about coming to Christ:

> *His love will find you and gently lead you*
> *From darkest night into day. . . .*
> *From ev'ry land and isle of the sea.*
> *Unto the high and lowly in station,*
> *Ever he calls, "Come to me."*

It seemed to me that we were all refugees together—all of us trying to flee from the world to the gospel of Jesus Christ, from error to truth. I felt so powerfully that unity in our need to come unto Jesus.

After the meeting I went over to Khanh, Rita's secretary, and began to talk to her. As soon as she began to talk, I began to cry, and I did so throughout our whole conversation, which lasted about half an hour. I felt sure the same would happen with every single person in the camp if I could speak to those people and hear their stories and think about who they really were and what they had been through. I found myself asking a question in my heart as I watched the refugees and tried to look into their faces: "Who are you?"

On Monday I returned to the camp and was once again immersed in the feelings of hope, ingenuity, and patience that surrounded me. I'd read many of the stories the missionaries had collected, and I was able to meet some of the people who had had those experiences. How was it, I wondered, that they could have so much peace when they had been treated with such terrible iniquity?

I had anticipated that the people in the camps would be angry and bitter, restless, anxious to get out and get going with their lives. There were so many thousands of them, with no privacy or personal space—things that seemed so important to me. Instead they were peaceful, respectful of each other, disciplined, and helpful. It was as if they were so close to freedom that they didn't want to do anything that might delay it, that might postpone or even destroy their dream.

Children gathered around us at every point and seemed very interested in trying to speak a little English to us. I loved watching the way they ran to the sisters, whom they saw every day. I was impressed with the bond of love that had developed, even though the sisters didn't know many words of the languages of the camp, and most of the people didn't speak or understand English.

One family we visited had used some of their twenty pieces of bamboo to build one bed off the floor so some things could be stored underneath, and then with the rest they had built a wall to help keep the rain out and give them a little privacy from the family right next to them. They had taken pictures and pages from magazines and put them on the walls. We took our shoes off and sat on the floor to visit with that family. The father had built a small bookshelf; on it was one old copy of the *National Geographic*.

As we were visiting, a little girl accidentally bumped into a small bag of rice, spilling it all over. Immediately, without any anger, the adults and children stopped what they were doing and helped to pick up every single piece of rice. I learned much from that simple act demonstrating the value of one precious kernel of rice. I thought of how much I must have wasted during my life that might have been of great worth to someone else.

I walked around the camp, watching the sisters teach the people. One of them let me take a few minutes in her class, which turned out to be a group of people who spoke Mandarin. I remembered a few words of that language and had a happy experience. At one point a young boy looked up at me and said, "You beautiful." I smiled and said, "You're beautiful too." He said, "How are you?" "Fine, how are you?" "I fine." He grinned and then said, "I Vietnam." I said, "I America." He asked, "Are you teacher?" I said, "Yes." Then he said, "You teacher, me student," and smiled. Oh no, I thought, You are my teacher. I recognized even before I arrived in the camp that I had much to learn and that I was surrounded by thousands of teachers. Those people had been through things I would never experience, and I wanted to know something of what they had learned and what they were feeling. I felt a sense of profound respect.

One little girl in an oversized pink shirt seemed to watch me constantly. I have no idea how old she was or who she was. Every time I looked directly at her to smile or communicate in some way, she ran away. She began to represent everyone to me—especially all the little children and what they'd been through. I wondered about her, who she was, and what she had experienced at her tender age.

Toward the end of the day we went back to the place where the missionaries had their office, and I sat leaning on the window with my back to the outside. My arms were stretched out, and my hand was on the edge of the window.

After a while I noticed the little girl in the pink shirt approaching me, walking very quietly, watching to see if I would turn around. I didn't. I just sat quietly, waiting to see what would happen. She got closer and closer. When she was right next to me she stopped. We were both very quiet. I didn't turn. Then she reached up, touched me, and ran. It was like electricity—that quick touch from a tiny finger. I felt it deep in my soul and was moved to tears.

I was still sitting there trying to handle that experience when I noticed that she was coming back. I still didn't turn; I once more waited to see what would happen. Again she approached carefully and quietly, and again she stood waiting. Once again she touched me and ran, and I felt a deep and powerful response.

She did that another time and I still didn't turn, so I think she decided I was dead or something. The last time she came and stood as before, but then she reached up and put her whole small hand on top of mine and pressed it hard. I wept; no, I sobbed. I was filled with love for that child and kept thinking, Oh, little child, who are you? Where are you from? Are your parents alive? Do you have any brothers and sisters? Are there people who care about you and are helping you? Where will you go? Where will you live? Will people be nice to you? Will they ever understand what you've gone through?

I wonder where she is now, that little girl in the pink shirt who affected me in such a permanent, significant way. Will I see her again someday?

On that day in Phanatnikom I thought about times when I had been frustrated about something or other, and those frustrations seemed rather insignificant and minimal at that moment in that place. I recognized that I had been blessed constantly and abundantly in my life, and there was so much good I could do if I would be willing. Every single soul on the earth has needs, but we also all have things to share. Those needs and those resources will likely vary at different times, in the different seasons of our lives.

I think of the phrase in "How Firm a Foundation": "As thy days may demand, so thy succor shall be." And it is. I have felt that strongly in my own life. God knows me— every single day. He knows my needs. I would like to be more that way with others. I'd like to help provide that succor, that refuge, that sense of safety and peace. I'd also like the very last words of that hymn to be true of me: "The soul that on Jesus hath leaned for repose . . . I'll never, no never, no never forsake!"

May we find those who are hungry, thirsty, sick, naked, strangers, or in any needy circumstance, and may we kindly, gently, honestly say to them: "You have come to the right place. You're safe now. This is a place where you can cry, ask, share feelings, and be understood." As we serve the least of these His children, may we know in our hearts that we have done it unto Him.

Chapter 12

CHARITY NEVER FAILETH

I REMEMBER HEARING AS a young child the phrase "charity never faileth." I knew it was somehow associated with Relief Society, and there was a time when I thought it meant, "Don't start a quilt unless you plan to finish it." I have since learned that it means much, much more than that. It is an important part of Relief Society and has been for many years. And as my own years and experiences have gone by, I have learned a lot more about what charity means and why it never fails.

Charity is a gift we can cultivate and pray for: the ability to love everyone everywhere in a Christlike, tender way. Charity—the pure love of Christ—is the greatest force on this earth, and the only thing powerful enough to change all the trouble in the world.

We find examples of charity in the scriptures. In Moroni 7, Mormon teaches what charity means to him. He defines it as pure love and points out that "if ye have not charity, ye are nothing, for charity never faileth. Wherefore, cleave unto charity, which is the greatest of all, for all things must fail—but charity is the pure love of Christ, and it endureth forever; and whoso is found possessed of it at the last day, it shall be well with him" (Moroni 7:46–47). What a promise! What a declaration about the importance of this quality, this depth of love that helps us to be good and to do good.

It was instructive for me to explore definitions of the words used in Moroni 7 and 1 Corinthians 13 to better understand charity. Let's look more closely at the list of qualities or characteristics of charity:

Charity suffereth long. To suffer is to endure, bear, allow, permit, tolerate. Job suffered long. So did Christ. So have countless others.

Charity is kind, friendly, gentle, tenderhearted, and generous.

Charity envieth not. There is no discontent or ill will because of another's advantages or possessions, no desire to get something that belongs to someone else.

Charity vaunteth not itself, does not brag or boast or seek to be above another. Was Christ teaching us of charity when He said, "He that is greatest among you shall be your servant"? (Matthew 23:11). Was He helping us know how to develop and exercise charity when He reminded us that serving others was as if we had done it unto Him? (Mosiah 2:17–22; Matthew 25:40). What about the Savior's message that every man should esteem his brother as himself (D&C 38:24–27) and that we should remember in all things the poor and the needy? (D&C 52:40). In deed as well as in word He pointed out that those who had should share with those who had not (Mosiah 18:27–28) and that those who were strong should help those who were weak (Romans 15:1). He asked us to feed His sheep—to act toward others as He, the Good Shepherd, would.

Charity is not puffed up. If we have charity, we do not want praise unduly. Trying to put ourselves above one another can make us tired and sick. We can't afford to separate ourselves from others. We need them as much as they need us.

Charity does not behave itself unseemly. We avoid that which is indecent or unbecoming.

Charity seeketh not her own. There are no exclusive groups—one possessed of the pure love of Christ reaches out to everyone. We visit those who can't come to visit us. We practice becoming better listeners. We speak to people we don't know yet, be the first to be friendly and to get acquainted. We work to have a countenance that shows love to everyone.

Charity is not easily provoked. If we have charity, we are patient and not easily angered or irritated. No small thing! This is one I have to work on continually. The real Christian is not touchy, doesn't have a quick temper, and is not impatient. Even when he or she is driving in traffic . . .

Charity thinketh no evil. Charitable people are always looking for the good in people, situations, experiences. We need to forgive each other. That is critical if we are to receive forgiveness and to have peace of mind ourselves.

Charity rejoices not in iniquity. We strive to purge wickedness from our lives and close the gap between our righteous desires and our actual behavior. We want to have the harmony and inner peace that come from forsaking evil.

Charity rejoiceth in the truth, in that which is established as fact, as principle. Those with charity strive to be true, sincere, genuine, honest, and in agreement with established standards.

Charity beareth all things. To bear means to undergo successfully, to be capable of withstanding, to permit, to sustain the burden of. It includes the lightening of others' burdens, helping to make their burdens bearable.

Charity believeth all things, having confidence in a statement or promise of another person, especially God.

Charity hopeth all things—a desire accompanied by anticipation, trust, or reliance.

Charity endureth all things—to last, continue, remain; to bear.

And finally, *charity never faileth*. Charity never lacks or falls short, never deceives or disappoints. It is never insufficient or negligent, never loses strength or power, is never useless or ineffectual, never abandons, leaves, or omits.

No wonder this pure love never fails! What a marvelous thing, to have something in our lives that will never fail, that will endure forever. So much in life does fail: our brakes, our teeth, our phones, our furnaces—even our hearts, and sometimes our relationships. Food spoils and treasures break and batteries wear out and something that was a great invention a few years ago has been replaced with something fancier, faster, and finer, but love—charity—never fails. It is and always will be constant and powerful.

How do we develop charity? It doesn't just happen after a certain number of years go by. We are commanded to pray for this gift, but then what are we willing to do? That's where we start: with our *willingness*. We are willing to bear one another's burdens, to mourn with them and comfort them, to take upon us the name of Jesus, to be Christians: Christlike, covenant people.

When we are willing to do loving, kind things, ideas come to us about when and why and how and to whom to do them. Where there's a will, there's a way. Christ has said, "I am the way," and we follow His example. He needs our help to show others the way to come unto Him.

Charity is not only the act, the doing, but that which compels us to act and to do—the tender, compassionate feeling in our soul that won't let us ignore someone who needs us. Charity is a condition of the heart and a conditioning of the heart. There are many ways we can develop and recognize charity in ourselves and others. We can consciously do things that bring more compassion and gentleness into our hearts and our actions. We learn about charity through our own experiences with sorrow as well as with joy. We can spend time with children who can help us to be more childlike, more charitable. After all, we're supposed to become as little children. And as we spend time with senior Saints, who many times feel neglected and forgotten, they can be tenderizers in our hearts and lives. They have much to teach us.

A few years ago I was doing a lot of thinking about becoming as a child. I decided that one way to help that happen would be to associate with little children as much as possible. I noticed a small boy about four or five years old playing in some sand across the street. I put on my grubbies and collected some of my toys and walked over there. "Can I play?" I asked. He looked up at me with a kind of squinting scrutiny. "Do you know how?" he wanted to know. I said, "I think so." So he let me play, and I remembered everything—what noises to make, how to build roads and bridges and ponds . . . it was a wonderful couple of hours.

We can respond cheerfully and willingly to opportunities for service. We can respond to those who have a need to give by accepting their help and kindness with gratitude and joy. Without gracious, grateful receivers, how will those who need and want to share have a chance to do so?

Charity is cooperation, teamwork, unselfish sharing of responsibilities and of the spotlight. It is love at home and kind words to one another. A woman who is a successful attorney said, "Charity just means that people love each other. And if people did love each other the way they should, it might not be good for my practice, but it would be good for the world."

We develop charity as we try to live more fully the law of the fast. This important law of God involves more than going without food and paying a minimum amount for meals missed. It means an offering of ourselves, not just of things or money. It is an act of genuine worship, a way to give thanks. It links responding to those who are hungry, thirsty, and needy with keeping our baptismal and other covenants. And oh, the promises! As we reach out to others, we will always find God there. Isaiah 58:6–12 explains it beautifully:

"Is not this the fast that I have chosen? to loose the bands of wickedness, to undo the heavy burdens, and to let the oppressed go free, and that ye break every yoke?

"Is it not to deal thy bread to the hungry, and that thou bring the poor that are cast out to thy house? when thou seest the naked, that thou cover him; and that thou hide not thyself from thine own flesh?

"Then shall thy light break forth as the morning, and thine health shall spring forth speedily: and thy righteousness shall go before thee; the glory of the Lord shall be thy rereward.

"Then shalt thou call, and the Lord shall answer; thou shalt cry, and he shall say, Here I am. If thou take away from the midst of thee the yoke, the putting forth of the finger, and speaking vanity;

"And if thou draw out thy soul to the hungry, and satisfy the afflicted soul; then shall thy light rise in obscurity, and thy darkness be as the noonday:

"And the Lord shall guide thee continually, and satisfy thy soul in drought, and make fat thy bones: and thou shalt be like a watered garden, and like a spring of water, whose waters fail not.

"And they that shall be of thee shall build the old waste places: thou shalt raise up the foundations of many generations; and thou shalt be called, The repairer of the breach, The restorer of paths to dwell in."

Some of the tenderest words in all of scripture are in those verses. As we seek to live the law of the fast, the Lord will guide us continually. Our darkness shall be as the noon-day. We will call to God, and He will answer. We will cry, and He will say, "Here I am."

The deeper our relationship with God, the more we will long to serve and love Him and to make ourselves ready for anything He needs us to do. As we come unto Christ we can turn and help others come to Him too. That is the mission and purpose of the Church and the gospel. The scriptures are the handbook of instructions for those who wish to love and serve the way the Savior did (and does), to become filled with charity.

Charity helps us become more tenderhearted toward each other, more willing to forgive freely and completely. It's an important way to lighten our own burdens as well as the burdens of others. We are often too hard on ourselves and others. If we spend time comparing, criticizing, competing, or condemning, we might miss opportunities for intimacy and forgiving and service and unity that would add a great deal to our lives.

It's a challenge to grow close when the world is so big and so many things seem to pull us apart. As one of my friends said, "Before we had an icebox, we went to the market more often and we visited there. Even with an icebox we visited when we went outside to get the ice. Now we don't even have to go outside: not only does our refrigerator keep things cold but it makes its own ice."

In many cultures the women still carry their clothing to a stream and visit while they wash. That is their daily news-paper, their chance to remain close to each other. Most of us don't go to the stream anymore. We don't go out into the backyard to hang the clothes on the line and visit with a neighbor while we work. We have fences and bushes and dryers—some of us don't even have backyards—and we don't seem as close to our neighbors as we once were.

We have lights that turn on and off automatically, microwave ovens, cruise control, videos and computers, automatic dishwashers . . . and what have we done with all the extra time that we've saved? Have we invested any of it in relationships? Even many games and activities tempt us to play alone, to be alone.

There may be someone today, right now, who is desperate for friendship, for kindness, for someone just to take time for them. Maybe that someone is you. Maybe you are one who has cried hard this past week, who is going through a difficult transition, who has felt desperately lonely, who has lost someone you loved, who has reached out only to feel that hearts and hugs have been withheld. Maybe you are one who hurt someone's feelings unintentionally, or maybe you're working hard on forgiving someone yourself.

What would happen if you called up a person you hadn't seen or talked to in a long time (maybe because you had some little misunderstanding, or your ward got divided, or the book club was disbanded, or you moved to a new neighborhood) and you said, "Let's go to the park! I've got the picnic if you've got the time. Wear grubbies, because they've got great teeter-totters and a sandpile."

I'm convinced there are ways we can open up to each other. It's a risk, yes, but oh, it's worth it. Why not forgive someone this week? (Perhaps even yourself.) Why not include this in your next fast: to ask the Lord to help you to reach out to someone, to be the first to say you're sorry, even if you feel something was not your fault. Is there someone who needs your forgiveness?

Elder Jeffrey R. Holland said: "We [accept Christ's gift] by joining in the work of forgiving sins. . . . 'My brother's burden which I must bear is not only his outward lot . . . but quite literally his sin. And the only way to bear that sin is by forgiving it. . . . Thus the call to follow Christ always means a call to share [in] the work of forgiving [others] their sins. Forgiveness is the Christlike suffering which it is the Christian's duty to bear.' (Dietrich Bonhoeffer, *The Cost of Discipleship*, 2d ed., New York: Macmillan, 1959, p. 100.) . . .

" . . . Anyone can be pleasant and patient and forgiving on a good day. A Christian has to be pleasant and patient and forgiving on all days. . . .

"Is there someone in your life who perhaps needs forgiveness? . . . All of us are guilty of . . . transgressions, so there surely must be someone who yet needs your forgiveness.

"And please don't ask if that's fair. . . . You and I know that what we plead for is mercy—and that is what we must be willing to give.

"Can we see the tragic and ultimate irony of not granting to others what we need so badly ourselves? . . . That is the demanding pathway of perfection" (*Ensign*, August 1986, p. 72).

In the greatest example we have of forgiveness, our Savior and Redeemer asked his Father to "forgive them; for they know not what they do." That was an act of charity, of pure love, like no other I can think of.

Can you think honestly that someone who has hurt or offended you might not have known what he or she was doing? Wouldn't it be wonderful to lift that burden—both from the offender and from you? "Blessed are the merciful: for they [you] shall obtain mercy" (Matthew 5:7).

Many of us wish others would forgive. Maybe we have suffered and struggled with trying to seek forgiveness and it just hasn't come. If that is the case for you, please don't give up. But please also don't fail to forgive yourself, even though at this time you don't seem to be receiving forgiveness from someone else. I am instructed by the reminder in Ephesians

4:32, "And be ye kind one to another, tenderhearted, forgiving one another, even as God for Christ's sake hath forgiven you." I am also heartened by the words of Thomas Erskine: "I believe that love reigns, and that love will prevail. I believe that He said to me every morning, 'Begin again thy journey and thy life: thy sins, which are many, are not only forgiven, but they shall be made, by the wisdom of God, the basis on which He will build blessings.'"

Charity will bring us together to work, to give thanks, to rejoice in the promise of living—our perfect brightness of hope. Charity will help qualify us to be with our heavenly family once again. Our Savior will help us. He understands when we can't do what we wish we could. God can heal all our wounds and help us with all our struggling. God the Father and his Son Jesus Christ can say, "I know just how you feel." They can help others feel Their love through us. They can help knit our hearts together in unity and love one toward another.

May God bless us with His Spirit and with the gift of charity, that it may be well with us when we see Him again. Charity never faileth. It never fails to move one soul to reach out to another. It never fails to come back and comfort and bless the one who has given. It never fails to give us the assurance that God lives and Christ is our Savior and that Their love for us is unconditional. No matter what, They will always love us. That pure love—charity—truly never fails.